One Pan Wonders
~ Backcountry Cooking at its Finest ~

By Teresa "Dicentra" Black

http://www.onepanwonders.com

For Maddy.

One Pan Wonders ~ Backcountry Cooking at its Finest
© Copyright 2008

All Rights Reserved.

ISBN 978-0-615-24676-5
First Printing August 2008

Cover photograph © copyright 2008, Sarah Kirkconnell.

Special thanks to:

In no particular order...

Shelby and James Buchanan for technical support.

Dad. For everything.

The PNWH for wanting to hike at a moment's notice, backcountry potlucks, recipe ideas, testing and a million other things. So many of the meals in this book are a direct result of hiking with all of you.

Sarah, for all the professional advice.

Team Osborne. You are like family.

My dear, patient husband. For believing I could do it. The dinner and dessert chapters would not be the same without your help.

Contents

Introduction

What is One Pan Wonders? How it all got started.

When I first started backpacking, I briefly ate freeze-dried dinners. I quickly discovered that they were a salt fest and just don't taste very good. The portion sizes were too big for me and the cost of them (for what you get) is ridiculous. I knew there had to be a better way.

I started looking at all of the backpacking cookbooks available and was disappointed. Most of the recipes either required a dehydrator or didn't offer meals that appealed to me. A lot of the recipes were also geared toward thru hiking. This is great, but I'm not a thru hiker. I don't need to worry as much about the weight of my pack when I am only going to be out for a few nights. I also didn't want to cook a full meal at home and then dehydrate it. To me, that was too much work for a weekend backpacking trip. I would rather just cook on the trail.

Talking to my buddies as we hiked, ideas started to flow. There were so many choices available right in the regular grocery stores. There was no reason for me not to start making my own backpacking meals at home.

One thing about living in the Seattle area is how lucky we are to have such an ethnically diverse population. The products available in our grocery stores reflect the Asian and Hispanic influences. For the purpose of this book, all of the ingredients included in the recipes are those which I could walk into a store and purchase. It is easy here to find unusual ingredients. I have a lot of fun incorporating these elements into my recipes. Some places don't have as many choices, so I have included a list of resources in the back of the book. Ordering from the internet has never been easier. It gives you unlimited meal possibilities that we have not had in the past.

About the Book

Serving/Portion sizes

Please read through the instructions completely. Serving sizes will vary depending on your own needs as well as the nutritional and/or caloric needs of your trip. In other words, on harder trips you will need more calories and bigger portions. A six foot tall man would probably eat twice as much as I would. Feel free to adjust the recipes to your own needs.

Nutritional information

I have not included nutritional information. I looked at several programs that compile this data, but I was unsatisfied with their results. They varied so much that I did not feel confident enough in their accuracy to include the information.

Temperatures/Elevation

All temperatures are in degrees Fahrenheit. All of the recipes were tested at or below 6000 feet. You may need to adjust cooking time and/or temperatures for higher elevations.

Equipment -Techniques, Gear and Tools

Freezer Bag Cooking and cozies

A cozy is something that will insulate your meal and keep it warm while it cooks and/or rehydrates. There are several commercial ones available, but a fleece or wool hat will also work. This method of cooking utilizes zip locking plastic bags and is generally called "Freezer Bag Cooking." For any of the meals listed in the book, if it is a just-add-water type of recipe, you may want to use a cozy in cold temperatures, even if the recipe doesn't specifically call for one. Cozies are also nice in the summer heat for keeping foods (like chocolate!) cool.

If you are hiking in bear country do not use clothing as a cozy unless you store it in your bear bag (canister) at night. Using a sleeping bag as a cozy would work, but I don't recommend it for the off chance you might spill food.

Zip locking plastic bags

These are mentioned throughout the book. I am referring to zip locking FREEZER bags. They are tougher and thicker than regular zip locking bags. They can withstand the jostling and bumping that happens in your pack. Use brand name freezer bags. The no-name brands aren't as good of quality.

Sharpie®

Use these to write directions and contents on your zip locking bags. Most freezer bags provide a white space on their surface for this purpose.

Kitchen kit – including stoves and pans

I currently have a Snow Peak Giga Power. I splurged and bought the titanium version with the auto start feature. This is a nice *quiet* stove, with an adjustable flame. And it is really light weight! One small fuel canister has lasted me for up to 6 days. The stove itself folds up into its storage box and fits inside my titanium mug. I just stick the fuel canister in my cooking pot, with the mug and a bandanna-wrapped pot gripper.

This has two purposes. One, it keeps the pot gripper from scratching my pot. And two, the bandana serves as a kitchen rag and/or a secondary potholder. I use it on every trip!

I used to have an MSR Dragonfly, and was never really happy with it. It was as noisy as a jet airliner. I did like that the flame could be adjusted and it had a much bigger base for my pot to sit on, so it was very stable. What I did NOT like was how often I would spill fuel on myself or the ground, causing a dangerous situation. This either happened when I was trying to refill the fuel bottle or trying to screw on the valve. And it was often hard to get the fuel valve screwed on just right. I usually cross threaded it. And with cold hands? Forget it!

I'm in the market for a new set of pans. I currently have the MSR (I do like MSR, just not that stove!) BlackLite Guide set. I've had this set for almost 10 years now and the non-stick coating is starting to come off. MSR has an excellent warranty on their cookware, but I know I've gotten my money's worth out of these pans! I won't be returning them. Just retiring them. GSI has a wonderful line of cookware and I will most likely buy something from them.

What else is in my kitchen? A small Swiss army knife, and a Snow Peak titanium spoon and fork set. I usually bring a bowl or a plate along too, and I have several to choose from. Depending on what I am cooking, my kitchen will also include zip locking plastic bags and small screw top containers. Except for the make-at-home recipes, you won't need anything more than those tools on the trail for this book's recipes.

Small screw top containers

They come in a variety of sizes, so you can choose one that fits your needs. These are excellent for bringing olive oil, vinegars and other liquids along on the trail. You can also carry peanut butter and salad dressings in them. Olive oil comes with me on every trip – day hike or backpack. A small screw top container is perfect for this.

Disclaimer

I am not a nutritionist, nor do I have any sort of professional training in food preparation. I am merely a hiker and backpacker that enjoys eating well and has taught herself how to cook, both in the backcountry and at home. The wilderness can be a dangerous place, as can cooking. Use caution to prevent burns, spills and other incidents while cooking in the backcountry. **I do not take any responsibility for the use of any materials or methods described in this book, on my website, nor of any products mentioned in them.**

Ingredient List

Bacon, Shelf Stable – Dried bacon bits may be substituted, but the flavor will not be the same. Look for shelf stable bacon in salad dressing aisle, usually with the croutons and other salad toppers. Most packages recommend refrigerating the opened package.

Beans, Dried – Look for soup or dip mixes in the bulk bins. Also available from Harmony House Foods.

Bulgur – A cereal, made from parboiled wheat. It is the traditional main ingredient in Tabbouleh. It has a nice nutty flavor and chewier texture. Look for it in bulk bins and "natural" food aisles. Substitute rice or couscous in most instances.

Coconut Crème Powder – Available at Asian markets and other online sources. Some brands use milk products in their processing, so if you are on a vegan diet, check the labels.

Coffee, Instant – There are so many choices for coffee on the trail now. Some are a lot better than others. Pick a good brand of instant coffee and you won't be sorry. You will have to experiment to find one you like. I use Trader Joe's freeze dried instant coffee for my mixes. I usually use the tea bag style coffee for my morning trail coffee though.

Couscous – Look for it in bulk bins or "natural" foods aisles. It is often found with rice mixes. I only use plain (not flavored or seasoned). Bulgur or instant rice make good substitutes, but cooking time may need to be adjusted.

Curry Powder – A blend of spices used in Indian cooking. Brands vary and may be mild or hot. Available in well stocked grocery stores and in bulk bins. Experiment until you find a blend that you like.

Gnocchi – Potato dumplings. These are made from a mashed potato like mixture. Great in soups and with sauces. They are very dense and filling. Look for the shelf stable version in the upper shelves of the pasta aisle. One fourth to one third of a package feeds one person easily. Pasta may be substituted, but you will have to adjust the cooking time.

Five Spice Powder – A combination of spices, usually star anise, ginger, cloves, cinnamon, and either peppercorns or fennel seeds. Recipes vary. It is available in bulk spice bins, in the spice or Asian food aisles of larger supermarkets, Asian grocery stores or online. You can also make your own blend from the individual spices.

Fruit, Dried – There are a lot of choices available; dried, freeze-dried, chocolate coated, yogurt covered. Trader Joe's is my favorite place to buy dried fruit. If that isn't an option for you, try the bulk bins or baking aisle. You can also find freeze-dried fruit online at Harmony House Foods or Just Tomatoes.

Meats and Seafood – In foil pouches or cans. Try the tuna and/or canned meats aisles of your grocery store. Chicken may not be in the same aisle as tuna. Different stores often carry different choices of canned and packaged meats, so shop around. Prices can vary widely as well.

Milk, Powdered – I almost exclusively use Nido® brand of powdered milk. It is a full fat powdered milk, and in my opinion, tastes a lot better than low fat powdered milk. It is available online at a variety of places or in the Hispanic food aisles of larger grocery stores. Milkman® is another brand that I sometimes use, but it does not dissolve well in hot liquids.

Mushrooms, Dried – There are several varieties available, ranging in price from ridiculously priced to very affordable. Shiitakes are available at Asian markets, larger grocery stores (Asian foods aisle) and online. Gourmet mushrooms (boletus, chanterelles, oysters etc) are available in larger grocery stores or online at Fungus Among Us and other online sources.

Nutella® – Chocolate hazelnut spread, the consistency of peanut butter, which it makes a good substitute for. Peanut butter is an adequate substitute in some cases. It is found in larger grocery stores, usually with the peanut butter. Trader Joe's and some import stores also carry it.

Nuts and Seeds – There are a lot of choices available. I like to get mine either in bulk bins or at Trader Joe's. They are also found in the baking aisle of most supermarkets. Seasoned/flavored varieties are appearing on the market now too. They add fat and protein to your meals without adding a whole lot of extra weight. Try different nuts than my recipes call for to add variety to your menus; pecans instead of walnuts, pine nuts in place of almonds. Your choices are virtually endless.

Potato Slices – Found in bulk bins or from a box of AuGratin potato mix (use the sauce for something else). Also available online from Harmony House Foods.

Salmon, Smoked – See also, Meats and Seafood. There are two kinds. I use both for different things. The flat, sheet kind is great for wraps and sandwiches. The filet kind is fantastic crumbled into pasta or rice dishes. Look for it in the seafood department. I don't recommend either type for hiking in bear country. A good substitution is a foil pouch of salmon.

Tofu – There are many types available. Experiment with tofu before you take it on the trail. Know how to cook it, and if you like it. I like the shelf-stable kind (Mori-Nu® brand) or the extra firm, refrigerated types – usually found in the produce section. It depends on what the recipe calls for, but I don't buy the type swimming in a lot of water. For dinner dishes, I use the firmer tofu. For desserts, such as puddings, I will use the softer, shelf stable variety. Baked tofu is excellent too. Try adding it to wraps or instant rice.

Tomatoes, Dried – See also, vegetables. There are two kinds of dried tomatoes; sun dried and freeze dried. Sun dried tomatoes are easier to find in grocery stores. Usually they are in the pasta aisle with the sauces. They also have a more complex flavor. Buy the kinds that are NOT packed in oil, but packaged in cellophane bags. They can be expensive, so shop around.

Tomato, Powder – available from Harmony House Foods. Knorr© soups also makes a version. It has a lot of flavor so a little bit goes a long way.

Tortillas – Readily found in most supermarkets. Try some of the "gourmet" flavors that are available now. Substitutions include pita bread, Flat Out Bread© and Mountain Bread®.

True Lemon/Lime/Orange – Substitute 1 teaspoon citrus juice or zest per packet. Available online at truelemon.com, minimus.biz and well stocked grocery stores.

TVP - Textured Vegetable Protein. I use plain, unflavored. Available in bulk bins, natural food stores, well stocked grocery stores or online. If you aren't used to eating TVP, start with small amounts as it can cause digestive issues. Some brands are better than others for rehydrating and flavor, so you may have to experiment a little to find one you like.

Vegetables, Dried – Look for soup mix in the bulk bins or Knorr© soups. Also available online from Harmony House Foods or Just Tomatoes.

Wasabi Powder – Wasabi paste or regular horseradish may be substituted. Available in Asian markets or in Asian food sections of larger grocery stores.

Breakfast

You NEED fuel in the morning. It warms you up, gets you going and gives you the energy you need to hit the trail. There is something special about sipping a cup of coffee while watching the sun come up and over an alpine ridge.

What you eat for breakfast depends on whether or not you want to have a leisurely start to your day. Do you mind fussing with dishes first thing in the morning? Or would you rather have a simple breakfast and break down camp quickly?

Oatmeal, rice, couscous, bulgur, instant cream of wheat and quinoa flakes are all interchangeable for instant type breakfasts. Try switching the varieties of nuts or dried fruits and the possibilities are virtually endless. Add more or less sugar and powdered milk to suit your own tastes.

For wraps and burritos, try the different varieties of flavored tortillas and other flat breads that are available now. Don't forget about pita bread, English muffins and bagels, which also pack well.

If you have coffee at home, don't forget about it when backpacking. On the trail is no place to get a lack-of-caffeine headache. If you don't want to fire up the stove in the morning, try chocolate covered coffee beans to get your pre-hike caffeine fix.

Peaches and Cream Oatmeal
Serves 1

1 packet plain instant oatmeal
3 tablespoons dried peaches, chopped
1 teaspoon cinnamon
2 tablespoons powdered milk
1/8 teaspoon ground nutmeg
1 tablespoon brown sugar (or to taste)

At home: combine everything in a zip locking plastic bag.

In camp: add 2/3 cup boiling water to oatmeal (or more if you like a thinner cereal.) Stir, let sit for 1 minute and eat!

Cherry Orange Pecan Oatmeal
Serves 1

1 packet plain instant oatmeal
2 packets True Orange©
2 tablespoons pecans, chopped
1 tablespoon dried cherries, chopped
1/4 teaspoon ground cinnamon
1 tablespoon powdered milk

At home: combine everything except the pecans in a zip locking plastic bag. Carry the pecans separately.

In camp: add 2/3 cup boiling water to oatmeal (or more if you like a thinner cereal.) Stir, top with pecans, let sit for 1 minute and eat!

Chai Oatmeal
Serves 1

If you like chai tea, you are going to love this! Try adding chopped dried apricots instead of the golden raisins.

1 packet plain instant oatmeal
2 tablespoons golden raisins
½ teaspoon ground cinnamon
¼ teaspoon ground coriander
¼ teaspoon ground allspice
1/8 teaspoon turmeric
1/8 teaspoon nutmeg
pinch of ground cloves
1 tablespoon brown sugar
1 tablespoon powdered milk

At home: combine everything in a zip locking plastic bag.

In camp: add 2/3 cup boiling water to oatmeal (or more if you like a thinner cereal.) Stir, let sit for 1 minute and eat!

AAA Oatmeal
Serves 1

1 packet plain instant oatmeal
1 tablespoon dried apricots, chopped
1 tablespoon dried apples, chopped
1 tablespoon almonds, chopped
½ teaspoon ground cinnamon
pinch nutmeg
1 teaspoon brown sugar
1 tablespoon powdered milk

At home: combine everything in a zip locking plastic bag.

In camp: add 2/3 cup boiling water to oatmeal (or more if you like a thinner cereal.) Stir, let sit for 1 minute and eat!

Creamy Mango Couscous
Serves 2-4

This would be good topped with chopped pecans.

1 cup couscous
¼ cup dried mango, finely diced
1 teaspoon powdered ginger
2 tablespoons brown sugar
4 tablespoons milk powder

At home: combine everything in a zip-locking plastic bag.

In camp: bring 2 cups of water to a boil. Add the contents of the bag stir, cover, remove from heat and let sit for 5-10 minutes or until the couscous is rehydrated. Fluff and eat.

Cranberry Couscous
Serves 1

1/4 cup couscous
2 tablespoons dried cranberries
1 teaspoon chopped pecans
1/4 teaspoon cinnamon
 pinch ground nutmeg
1 tablespoon powdered milk (or to taste)
1 tablespoon brown sugar (or to taste)

At home: combine everything in a zip locking plastic bag.

In camp: add enough water to cover, stir well and let sit for 5 minutes. Stir again and enjoy.

Bulgur with Pears
Serves 1

¼ cup bulgur
2 tablespoons dried pears, chopped
¼ teaspoon cinnamon
1/8 teaspoon nutmeg
1 teaspoon brown sugar
Powdered milk to taste

At home: combine everything in a zip locking plastic bag.

In camp: bring ½ cup of water to a boil and add the bulgur. Simmer until the bulgur is tender. Eat!

Blueberry Bulgur
Serves 1

¼ cup bulgur
2 tablespoons dried blueberries
1 teaspoon dried apples, chopped
1 tablespoon powdered milk
1 teaspoon brown sugar

At home: combine everything in a zip locking plastic bag.

In camp: bring ½ cup of water to a boil and add the bulgur. Simmer until the bulgur is tender. Eat!

Cinnamon Apple Spice Bulgur
Serves 1

1/4 cup bulgur
3 tablespoons dried apples, chopped
1 tablespoon chopped pecans
1/2 teaspoon cinnamon
1/4 teaspoon nutmeg
pinch ground cloves
1 tablespoon powdered milk
1 teaspoon brown sugar

At home: combine everything in a zip locking plastic bag.

In camp: place bag in a cozy. Add about 1/2 cup water (enough to cover). Stir and let stand for 5 minutes or until bulgur is tender.

Pina Colada Breakfast Rice
Serves 1

1/4 cup instant rice
1 dried pineapple ring, chopped (about 2 tablespoons)
1 tablespoon chopped macadamia nuts (optional)
1 tablespoon coconut crème powder
1 1/2 tablespoons powdered milk
2 teaspoons brown sugar (or to taste)

At home: combine everything in a zip locking plastic bag.

In camp: add enough hot water to cover; about 1/2 cup. Stir. Let stand for 5 minutes, or until rice is tender. Top with macadamia nuts before eating.

Blueberries and Cream Rice
Serves 1

1/4 cup instant rice
2 tablespoons dried blueberries
1/2 teaspoon cinnamon
1 teaspoon powdered milk
1 teaspoon brown sugar

At home: combine everything in a zip locking plastic bag.

In camp: add enough hot water to cover the rice. Stir. Set aside for 5 minutes or until rice is tender.

Golden Orange Spiced Rice
Serves 1

1/4 cup instant rice
2 packets True Orange©
2 tablespoons golden raisins
1 tablespoon chopped pecans
1 tablespoon powdered milk
1/4 teaspoon ground cinnamon
1/8 teaspoon allspice
1/8 teaspoon nutmeg
1 packet honey

At home: combine everything except the honey and pecans in a zip locking plastic bag. In a snack-sized plastic bag, place the pecans and honey. Put this bag in the rice bag.

In camp: remove the pecans and honey from the rice bag. Add enough hot water to cover. Stir. Set aside for 5 minutes, or until rice is tender. Top with honey and pecans before eating.

Variation: try chopped, dried apricots in place of the golden raisins.

Sunrise Bowl
Serves 1

½ cup instant cornmeal
½ cup dried apples, chopped
2 tablespoons dried cranberries
2 tablespoons chopped pecans
1 tablespoon brown sugar
½ teaspoon cinnamon
1 single serving packet of butter

At home: combine cornmeal, apples, cinnamon, brown sugar and cranberries in a zip locking plastic bag. Carry the pecans and butter separately.

In camp: bring 2 ¼ cups water to a boil. Gradually add the polenta. Stir, then cover and simmer until done. Top with pecans and butter.

10 Grain Apple Walnut Cereal
Serves 1

When I was testing this recipe, my daughter stole my spoon and wouldn't give it back. She ate most of my breakfast! So I guess it is safe to say that even kids like this.

1/2 cup 10-grain cereal
1/4 cup dried apples, chopped
1/4 cup walnuts
1 apple-cinnamon tea bag
1 tablespoon brown sugar
2-3 tablespoons powdered milk

At home: combine the cereal, apples, brown sugar and powdered milk in a zip locking plastic bag. You can place the tea in the bag too. Carry the walnuts in a separate bag. (You can add them to the cereal if you'd like, but if you add them AFTER the cereal is cooked, they stay crunchy.)

In camp: combine the tea bag and 1 1/2 cups of water. Bring to a boil. Remove the tea bag. Add the cereal and apples. Stir well. Simmer for a minute or two until the cereal is the consistency you want. Top with walnuts and enjoy!

Apple Breakfast Wrap
Serves 1

This can be made at home and wrapped up to go or made in camp.

1 whole wheat tortilla
¼ cup dried apples, chopped
2 tablespoons peanut butter
1 single serving packet of honey
½ teaspoons cinnamon

Spread peanut butter on the tortilla. Drizzle with the honey, and then sprinkle on the cinnamon. Top with the chopped apples. Roll and eat.

PB Crunch Wrap
Serves 1

This can be made at home and wrapped up to go or made in camp.

1 large flour tortilla
1/4 cup granola with dried fruit (your favorite)
2 tablespoons peanut butter
2 tablespoons jam or jelly

Spread the peanut butter on half of the tortilla. Spread the jelly on the other half. Top with the granola. Roll and eat.

Basic Breakfast Burrito
Serves 1

2 fresh eggs
2 2-ounce slices Swiss cheese
1 large flour (flavored or not) tortilla
1 tablespoon olive oil

At home: put the eggs in a hiking/backpacking egg carrier.
Put the cheese in a zip locking plastic bag. Carry the olive oil in a screw top container.

In camp: add oil to your pan. Scramble the eggs until cooked.
Put the eggs on the tortilla, top with cheese. Roll and eat.

Peanut Butter Chocolate Chip Pancakes
Serves 2

1 cup pancake mix (the just-add-water kind)
3 tablespoons mini chocolate chips
3 tablespoons peanut butter
2-3 tablespoons vegetable oil
jam or syrup

At home: combine the pancake mix and chocolate chips in a zip locking plastic bag. Carry the peanut butter and vegetable oil in separate screw top containers.

In camp: add ¾ cup water, and then the peanut butter to the pancake mix. Squish the bag until well combined. Heat oil in pan. Drop batter by tablespoonfuls into the pan. Flip when bubbles form on top of the pancakes. They cook fast, so watch carefully. Be sure to scoop to the bottom of the bag as the chocolate chips have a tendency to sink. Serve topped with jam or syrup.

Hoh Cakes
Serves 1-2

Let the kids help! My daughter loves to squish the bag for me. Just make sure it is sealed well before you hand it over.

¾ cup cornmeal (polenta)
¼ cup Bisquick©
1 teaspoon sugar (optional)
3-4 tablespoons vegetable oil
syrup or jam

At home: combine the cornmeal, Bisquick© and sugar in a zip locking plastic bag. Carry the oil in a screw top container.

In camp: add ¾ cup water to the cornmeal mix. Seal the bag and squish until there are no lumps. It should be about the consistency of pancake batter. Heat a little oil in your pan (just enough to coat the bottom – you want cakes not donuts). Drop the batter by tablespoonfuls into the pan, smoothing it out so it is not more than ¼ inch thick. Don't make them more than 2-3 inches across or they will be difficult to flip. When bubbles form on top, flip and fry the other side; about 30 seconds per side). Serve topped with syrup or jam.

Save some to eat with dinner!

Green and Gold Tofu Scramble
Serves 2

Adjust the seasonings, salt and pepper to your taste. My daughter LOVES this dish. Toddler approved! You can use scissors or kitchen shears to cut up the mushrooms and sun-dried tomatoes. The turmeric will turn the tofu a sunny, yellow color, making them look like scrambled eggs.

8 ounces firm tofu
1/2 cup spinach, well packed
2 tablespoons sun-dried tomatoes, NOT in oil, cut in small pieces
2 tablespoon dried mixed mushrooms, broken up
1-2 packets of soy sauce (1-2 tablespoons)
1/2 teaspoon turmeric
1 teaspoon dried oregano
1 tablespoon olive oil

At home: put the spinach in a zip locking plastic bag. In a second bag place the tomatoes, mushrooms, oregano and turmeric. Carry the olive oil in a screw top container. Carry the soy sauce separately.

In camp: heat the oil in your pan. Add the tofu, breaking it up with a fork. Cook until the tofu starts to turn golden brown. Add 1/2 cup of water, and the mushroom/tomato/spice mixture. Simmer long enough to rehydrate the vegetables (just a minute or two). Add the spinach and soy sauce just before serving.

Lunches, Snacks and Trail Mix

I don't usually do a regular lunch on the trail. I snack. I nibble. I munch. There are only two things that you will find in my pack on every trip; dark chocolate and dried mangoes. Everything else varies.

On cold winter hikes or snowshoeing trips, it is sometimes nice to take the time to cook a hot lunch and make a cup of tea or hot chocolate. Look to the dinner recipes for hot lunch ideas. I've kept the recipes in the lunch section stove-free.

Wraps can be made with a variety of breads. There are all kinds of different flavored tortillas available now. Have fun experimenting. Pita bread, Flat Out Bread© and Mountain Bread® are other possible substitutions. I like wraps because they are portable and you can eat them with one hand. Less mess and clean up as well. You won't have any dishes to wash with a wrap.

I have not included any granola recipes in this book. There is a wide variety of really good granola available. Find one you like. Frankly, I am not very good at making granola, but I do like eating it. There are several kinds I buy on a regular basis.

I feel likewise about trail bars. There are so many appetizing choices; I would rather not make my own. Laziness? Maybe. But I still eat well on trips.

Trail mix, however, I do like to make myself. I can control the ingredients and the proportions. Omit the ingredients you don't like and feel free to add your own favorites. Vary the nuts, seeds and dried fruits until you find a mix that is perfect for you. I find it is better to make mixes in small batches for two reasons. First, I like variety. I rarely take the same mix twice. Second, you end up with a fresher product, assuming you start with fresh ingredients. The bulk bins in larger supermarkets are your best friend for custom trail mixes. Buy whatever you want in tiny quantities, and get creative!

Dip mixes can double as a spread for sandwiches or wraps. I like to bring crackers, pita chips or vegetable sticks along for dipping. A little bit of mix goes a long way. Dip mixes can also be tossed with hot pastas for dinner. In addition to the just-add-water dips and spreads available in stores, it is easy to customize your own for the trail with the addition of a few simple ingredients.

Hula Wraps
Serves 2

This can be made on the trail, or at home before your hike.

2 large flour tortillas
1 3-ounce foil package tuna
2 individual packages cream cheese
2 rings dried pineapple, finely chopped
4 tablespoons macadamia nuts, finely chopped
1 tablespoon dried parsley
½ teaspoon curry powder

At home: combine the dried pineapple, macadamia nuts, parsley and curry powder in a zip locking plastic bag. Wrap the tortillas in foil or plastic wrap. Carry the cream cheese separately.

In camp: unwrap the tortillas; spread one package of cream cheese on each. Top with the pineapple and macadamia nuts and half of the tuna. Roll and eat!

Wasabi Tuna Wrap
Serves 1

This is designed to be made at home, but there is no reason you couldn't make it on the trail.

1 large flour or spinach tortilla
1 3-ounce foil package of tuna or salmon
1 cup fresh spinach
2 scallions, finely chopped
¼ teaspoon wasabi paste
1 tablespoon soy sauce

In a small bowl, combine the wasabi, soy sauce, scallions and tuna. Top the tortilla with the mixture. Top this with the spinach. Fold and wrap burrito-style and then wrap in plastic wrap or foil.

Cheery Cherry Chicken Wrap
Serves 1-2

2 large flour tortillas
4 2-ounce slices Swiss cheese
1 4.5-ounce can Underwood© white meat chicken
¼ cup dried cherries, chopped

Spread half of the chicken on each of the tortillas. Top with half of the dried cherries. Place 2 slices of cheese on each. Roll and wrap in foil or plastic wrap. Alternately, you can package the ingredients separately and assemble the wrap on the trail.

Apple Cheddar Wrap
Serves 1

This can be assembled at home or on the trail.

1 large flour tortilla
1 tablespoon honey mustard (or ½ tablespoon honey, ½ tablespoon Dijon mustard)
½ crisp apple, sliced thin
2 ounces smoked cheddar, sliced

Spread the honey mustard on the tortilla. Top with the apple slices, then the cheese. Roll and eat!

Cuban Burritos
Serves 1

1 large flour tortilla (flavored or not)
2 tablespoons dried tomatoes
¼ cup dried black beans (soup or dip mix)
1/2 teaspoon chili powder
¼ teaspoon ground cumin
1 packet True Lime©
1 packet (2 tablespoons) cream cheese

At home: combine the tomatoes, black beans, chili powder, cumin and True Lime© in a zip locking plastic bag. Wrap the tortilla in foil. Carry the cream cheese separately.

In camp: add just enough water to cover the tomatoes and black beans. Stir and set aside to rehydrate. Meanwhile, spread the cream cheese on the tortilla. When the beans and tomatoes are rehydrated, top the cream cheese with them. Wrap and eat.

Ford Wraps
Serves 1-2

My little hiking buddy loves these.

1 package smoked salmon (the kind in sheets)
2 single serving packages cream cheese
2 large flour or spinach tortillas

At home: wrap the tortillas in foil. Carry the cream cheese and salmon separately.

In camp: spread one package of cream cheese on each of the tortillas.
Put half of the salmon on each. Roll and eat.

Ranch Chicken Wrap
Serves 2

This can be made at home or on the trail.

2 large flour tortillas
1 3.5-ounce can Underwood© chicken or 1 3-ounce can chicken
¼ cup shredded carrots
¼ cup fresh spinach
1 2-ounce container ranch dressing (or 3 tablespoons, carried in a screw top container)
2 tablespoons sunflower seeds

Spread each of the tortillas with half of the chicken. Top with half of the sunflower seeds, then half of the carrots and spinach. Drizzle half of the ranch dressing over the spinach. Roll and eat (or wrap up to go.) Repeat with the remaining ingredients.

Black Bean Wrap
Serves 1

¼ cup instant black bean dip mix
2 packets True Lime© (optional)
¼ teaspoon dried cilantro
pinch red pepper flakes
1-2 packets hot sauce or salsa (from a take-out place)
1 2-ounce stick cheddar or pepper jack cheese
1 large flour tortilla

At home: combine the beans, True Lime©, cilantro and red pepper flakes in a zip locking plastic bag. Wrap the tortilla in foil or plastic wrap. Carry the hot sauce and cheese separately.

In camp: add about ¼ cup of water to the beans. Stir and allow to rehydrate. It should be a spread or dip like consistency. Spread on the tortilla, top with the cheese stick and hot sauce. Roll and eat.

Variation: to make this a dinner recipe, add some cooked rice and use hot water to rehydrate the beans.

Corn and Bean Salad
Serves 1

1/4 cup dried black beans (soup or dip mix)
2 tablespoons dried corn
1 teaspoon dried bell pepper
1 packet True Lime©
1/4 teaspoon ground cumin
1 teaspoon olive oil

At home: combine everything in a zip locking plastic bag.

In camp: add enough water to cover. Stir and allow to rehydrate before adding the olive oil.

Apple Bean Salad
Serves 1

¼ cup dried kidney beans (soup mix)
2 tablespoons dried apples, chopped
1 teaspoon dried celery or ¼ teaspoon celery seeds
1 teaspoon olive oil
1 teaspoon cider vinegar
½ teaspoon onion flakes
½ teaspoon chili powder

At home: combine all of the dry ingredients in a zip locking plastic bag. Combine the oil and vinegar in a screw top container.

In camp: add just enough water to the beans to cover. When almost rehydrated, add the oil and vinegar. Stir well before eating.

Sun-dried Tomato and White Bean Salad
Serves 1

¼ cup dried white beans (soup mix)
¼ cup fresh spinach
2 tablespoons sun-dried tomatoes, chopped (not oil packed)
1 packet True Lemon©
½ teaspoon dried oregano
 1 tablespoon olive oil
salt and pepper to taste

At home: combine all of the ingredients except the spinach and oil in a zip locking plastic bag. Carry the spinach in a second bag and the oil in a screw top container.

In camp: add enough water to the beans to cover. When almost rehydrated, add the oil and spinach. Stir well before eating.

Alternately, you can serve the bean salad on top of the spinach.

Orange Chicken Tabbouleh Salad
Serves 1-2

¼ cup bulgur
1 3-ounce can chicken
2 teaspoons dried mixed vegetables
2 packets True Orange©
1 teaspoon dried parsley
½ teaspoon onion flakes
¼ teaspoon dried mint
1 tablespoon olive oil

At home: combine all of the dry ingredients in a zip locking plastic bag. Carry the oil in a screw top container and the chicken separately.

In camp: add just enough water to cover. When almost rehydrated, add the oil and chicken (do not drain). Stir well before eating.

Variation: This can also be served in a pita or rolled in a tortilla.

White Bean Tuna Salad
Serves 1

1/3 cup dried white beans (soup mix)
1 3-ounce foil package tuna
½ teaspoon dried parsley
½ teaspoon dried oregano
¼ teaspoon onion flakes
1 packet True Lemon©
pinch red pepper flakes
1-2 tablespoons olive oil (optional)
salt and pepper to taste

At home: combine the beans and herbs in a zip locking plastic bag. Place the foil package of tuna in the bag. Carry the olive oil in a screw top container.

In camp: remove the foil packet of tuna from the bag. Add just enough water to cover the beans; about 1/3 cup. Let stand for 5 minutes, and then stir in tuna and olive oil. Eat warm or cold.

Chicken Salad with Corn
Serves 1

This can be eaten as is, or served on crackers or pita bread.

1 3-ounce can chicken
1 tablespoon dried tomatoes
1 tablespoon dried corn
½ teaspoon ground coriander
½ teaspoon dried basil
½ teaspoon dried parsley
¼ teaspoon ground cumin
¼ teaspoon onion flakes
1 tablespoon olive oil
½ tablespoon balsamic vinegar
salt and pepper to taste

At home: combine all of the dry ingredients in a zip locking plastic bag. Combine the olive oil and balsamic vinegar in a screw top container. Carry the chicken separately.

In camp: add enough water (hot or cold) to cover the vegetables. When almost rehydrated, add the chicken and oil and vinegar. Stir well and eat.

Fremont Hash
Serves 1

¼ cup bulgur
2 tablespoons plain TVP
5 dried apricots, chopped
1 teaspoon vegetable bouillon
1 packet True Lemon©
1 teaspoon dried basil
½ teaspoon dried mint
1 teaspoon dried parsley

At home: combine everything in a zip locking plastic bag.

In camp: add just enough water to cover. Stir well to combine. Set aside for about 10 minutes and allow to rehydrate. Stir, add more water if necessary and eat.

Vegan Instant Lunch
Serves 1

¼ cup bulgur
2 tablespoons plain TVP
1 tablespoon dried shiitake mushrooms, broken up
1 tablespoon dried corn
1 tablespoon dried carrot
1 tablespoon dried parsley
¼ teaspoon dried basil
½ teaspoon dried onion flakes
1 teaspoon vegetable bouillon
salt and pepper to taste

At home: combine everything in a zip locking plastic bag.

In camp: add just enough water to cover. Squish the bag to make sure the water gets distributed evenly. Set aside for 5 minutes to rehydrate. Add more water if needed. Stir and eat.

Lodge Lake Tapenade
Serves 1-2

I like whole grain Wasa© crackers with this.

½ cup dried white beans (soup mix)
1 tablespoon dried tomatoes
1 tablespoon dried parsley
1 teaspoon dried onion flakes
1 packet True Lemon©
½ teaspoon ground cumin
salt and pepper to taste
crackers

At home: combine everything in a zip locking plastic bag.

In camp: add just enough water to cover. Squish the bag to make sure the water gets distributed evenly. Set aside for 5 minutes to rehydrate. Squish bag again and spoon the tapenade onto crackers to serve.

Split Pea Dip
Serves 1-2

1/3 cup split pea soup mix
1 tablespoon olive oil
1/2 teaspoon dried onion flakes
1/2 teaspoon dried oregano
1/8 teaspoon garlic powder
salt and pepper to taste

At home: combine all of the dry ingredients in an airtight container. I like small plastic bowls with lids because I can make the dip right in them on the trail. Carry the olive oil in a screw top container.

In camp or on the trail: add about 1/4 cup water. Let sit for about a minute before adding the olive oil. Serve on crackers, pita bread or carrot sticks.

Orange Spice Hummus
Makes about 6 servings (2 tablespoons each)

½ cup instant hummus mix
4 packets True Orange©
1 teaspoon dried parsley
¼ teaspoon paprika
¼ teaspoon ground coriander
1/8 teaspoon ground ginger
1/8 teaspoon ground cumin
1/8 teaspoon turmeric
1-2 tablespoons olive oil (optional)

At home: combine everything in a zip locking plastic bag or other air tight container.

In camp or on the trail: add water and stir until you get the consistency you desire. If you are making the whole recipe, you will want about ¾ cup water. Stir well. The dip thickens as it sits, but you can add more water to thin it out. Serve on pita, crackers or carrot sticks.

Smokey Crackers
Serves 1-2

Smoked oysters are also available in foil pouches. Look for them to save a little weight on this recipe.

1 3.75-ounce can smoked oysters
4 ounces smoked cheddar cheese, sliced
crackers of your choice (plain is better)

At home: put the cheese and crackers in separate zip locking plastic bags. Carry the oysters separately.

In camp or on the trail: top crackers with sliced cheese and then the oysters.

Pumpkin Cranberry Energy Bars
Makes 1 dozen

These are good for breakfast or dessert on the trail. Try spreading them with cream cheese. Yams or sweet potatoes can be substituted for the pumpkin

½ cup water
½ cup rolled oats
1 16-ounce can cooked pumpkin puree
½ cup cornmeal
¼ cup honey
2 teaspoons cinnamon
1 teaspoon ground ginger
¼ teaspoon nutmeg
1/8 teaspoon ground cloves
1 egg
¼ cup dried cranberries
¼ cup finely chopped walnuts

Preheat oven to 350°F.

Combine the oats with the water. Let stand for 5 minutes. Add the pumpkin, cornmeal, honey, spices and egg.

Mix well. Add the cranberries and walnuts, stirring to just combine.

Drop, from a spoon, onto an oiled cookie sheet and smooth out the tops with the back of the spoon. The cakes should be about 3 inches in diameter.

Bake at 350°F for 25-30 minutes, turning once. Cool. Wrap individually in waxed paper.

Wasabi Almonds
Makes 1 pound

These will warm you up! Try with different types of nuts.

1 pound raw almonds
3 tablespoons wasabi powder
1 egg white
1 tablespoon water
2 teaspoons salt
2 teaspoons cornstarch
pinch black pepper

Preheat oven to 275°F. Line a cookie sheet with aluminum foil. Whisk egg white and water together, then add almonds and toss to coat. Place almonds in a sieve and allow to drain.

Place the wasabi powder, cornstarch and salt in a large zip locking plastic bag. Add the almonds and toss or squish to coat evenly. Spread the almonds on the cookie sheet in a single layer and bake for 30 minutes, watching carefully.

Stir gently. Lower heat to 200°F and continue baking for another 20 minutes. Let cool completely. Break apart if needed.

Take what you need for the trail in a zip locking plastic bag. Store the rest in an airtight container.

Cherry Pistachio Bark
Makes about 2 cups

This is really pretty. Adjust the amounts to your liking.

2 cups white chocolate chips
¼ cup dried cherries, chopped
¼ cup shelled pistachios, chopped
more dried cherries and pistachios to top (optional)

Line a cookie sheet with foil. Melt white chocolate in the microwave at 20 second intervals, stirring between each until thoroughly melted. Stir in the cherries and pistachios.

Spread the mixture out evenly on the foil. Top with more dried cherries and pistachios. Place in refrigerator and allow to cool. Break/cut into bite-sized pieces. Store in a zip locking plastic bag. Enjoy - on the trail or at home!

Sweet Caribbean Crunch
Makes 2 ½ cups

1 1/2 cups white chocolate chips or melting chocolate
1/4 cup cashews, chopped
1/4 cup dried mangoes, chopped
1/4 cup dried pineapple, chopped
1/4 cup shredded coconut

Combine the cashews, mangoes, pineapple and coconut.

Melt chocolate in the microwave in a large glass bowl (30 seconds at a time - stirring each time until thoroughly melted). Stir in dried fruit and coconut. Stir until well combined. Spread onto a cookie sheet lined with foil. Place in the refrigerator or freezer until fully set. Break into bite-sized pieces. Store in zip locking plastic bags for snacking on the trail.

Kelcema Lake Trail Mix
Makes 3 cups

1 cup dried cranberries
3/4 cup mini chocolate chips
3/4 cup salted almonds
1/2 cup white chocolate chips

Mix everything together and store in a zip locking plastic bag. Eat by the handfuls.

Esmeralda's Mix
Makes 1 1/2 cups

1/4 cup sunflower seeds
1/4 cup pine nuts
1/4 cup spicy dry roasted pumpkin seeds
1/4 cup golden raisins
1/4 cup dried cranberries

Combine everything in a zip locking plastic bag. Munch by the handfuls.

Owyhigh Mix
Makes 1 1/2 cups

1/4 cup golden raisins
1/4 cup pistachios (shelled)
1/4 cup dried mango, chopped
1/4 cup pumpkin seeds
1/4 cup sunflower seeds
1 pineapple ring, chopped

Combine everything in a zip locking plastic bag. Munch by the handfuls.

Peanut Crunch Mix
Makes 3 cups

1 cup peanut butter coated pretzels
1 cup peanut butter filled pretzels
1/2 cup dry roasted peanuts
1/4 cup peanut butter chips
1/4 cup raisins

Combine everything in a zip locking plastic bag. Munch by the handfuls.

Raspberry Chai Crunch
Serves 1

¼ cup dried raspberries
1 1.5-ounce oats and honey crunchy granola bar (both bars in the package)
1 teaspoon instant chai tea

At home: break up the granola bar into a zip locking plastic bag. Add the dried raspberries and then the chai tea. Shake well to coat the raspberries and granola.

In camp or on the trail: Munch!

Peanut Butter, Bananas and Chocolate
Makes about 1 cup

1 1.5-ounce peanut butter crunchy granola bar (both bars in the package)
¼ cup mini chocolate chips
¼ cup banana chips

At home: break up the granola bar and banana chips in a zip locking plastic bag.
Add the chocolate chips and shake well to distribute.

In camp or on the trail: Munch!

Asian Blend
Makes 1 1/2 cups

½ cup sesame sticks
¼ cup seaweed wrapped rice crackers
¼ cup wasabi peas
¼ cup salted soy nuts
¼ cup sunflower seeds

Combine everything in a zip locking plastic bag. Munch by the handfuls.

Goin' Fishin'
Makes 1 ½ cups

1 cup plain fish crackers
¼ cup sesame sticks
¼ cup salted mixed nuts

Combine everything in a zip locking plastic bag. Munch by the handfuls.

Naches Mix
Makes 3/4 cup

¼ cup freeze dried corn
¼ cup salted soy nuts
¼ cup pine nuts
1 teaspoon chili powder
¼ teaspoon dried oregano
¼ teaspoon ground cumin

Combine everything in a zip locking plastic bag. Munch by the handfuls.

Royal Lake Mix
Makes 1 3/4 cups

1/4 cup golden raisins
1/4 cup dried cranberries
1/4 cup sunflower seeds
1/4 cup pistachios (shelled)
1/4 cup dried cherries
1/2 cup cashews

Combine everything in a zip locking plastic bag. Munch by the handfuls.

Happy Hawaiian
Makes about 1 cup

1/4 cup macadamia nuts, coarsely chopped
1/4 cup dried pineapple, chopped
1/4 cup chocolate chips
1/4 cup dried mango, chopped
3 tablespoons crystallized ginger (optional)

Combine everything in a zip locking plastic bag. Munch by the handfuls

Soups and Chowders

The only thing better than eating soup on a cold night, is eating soup on a cold night in the backcountry. There is nothing like sipping a warm cup of soup after the tent is set up and the sun is dipping below the horizon or behind the mountains.

Soup can be as simple as a broth that you sip while the rest of your dinner is cooking, or it can be a hearty and filling main course. It is a great way to get extra fluids in at the end of the day, while keeping you warm at the same time. On cold winter nights, you will want those extra calories to keep warm.

Soups are also a great hot lunch option for fall/winter hikes or snowshoe trips. The little bit of extra mid-day warmth is a great pick-me-up to keep you going for the rest of the day.

If you are planning on having a rich dessert, then soups are a great choice for your main entrée at dinner time. I will often pair a soup, such as Mushroom Tortellini, with chocolate mousse or cheesecake for dessert. The result is very filling.

Black Bean Soup with Sherry
Serves 1-2

1 cup dried black beans (soup or dip mix)
2 tablespoons powdered milk
1 teaspoon chicken or vegetable bouillon
1 teaspoon ground cumin
1 teaspoon onion flakes
salt and pepper to taste
2 tablespoons dry sherry

At home: combine all of the dry ingredients in a zip locking plastic bag. Carry the sherry in a screw top container.

In camp: bring 1 cup of water to a boil. Add the bean soup mix, and then the sherry. Simmer until the beans are rehydrated and the soup is heated through.

Instant Minestrone
Serves 1

1 tablespoon couscous
1 tablespoon mixed vegetables
1 tablespoon dried kidney beans (soup mix)
1 teaspoon dried tomatoes
1 teaspoon chicken or vegetable bouillon
1/2 teaspoon tomato powder
1/4 teaspoon dried basil
1/8 teaspoon dried oregano
1/8 teaspoon garlic powder

At home: combine everything in a zip locking plastic bag.

In camp: add 1 to 1 1/4 cups hot water. Stir. Let stand 5 minutes before eating.

Three Sisters Stew
Serves 1

The dried vegetables can be purchased from Just Tomatoes or Harmony House Foods.

1/3 cup dried diced zucchini
1/3 cup dried corn
1/3 cup dried kidney beans (soup mix)
1/4 cup instant rice
1 teaspoon ground cumin
1 teaspoon onion flakes
1/2 teaspoon garlic powder
1/2 tablespoon vegetable or chicken bouillon
 salt and pepper to taste

At home: combine everything in a zip locking plastic bag.

In camp: add enough water to cover. Allow the beans and vegetables to rehydrate. Add more water to get the consistency you desire.

Black Bean and Corn Chicken Chili
Serves 1

1 3-ounce can chicken
1/4 cup dried black beans (soup mix)
1 tablespoon dried tomatoes
1 tablespoon dried corn
1 teaspoon chili powder
1/2 teaspoon onion flakes
1/4 teaspoon garlic powder
pinch red pepper flakes (or more to taste)

At home: combine all of the ingredients except the chicken in a zip locking plastic bag. Carry the chicken separately.

In camp: add enough hot water to cover. Let stand for 5 minutes until the beans and vegetables are rehydrated. Add more water if needed to get the consistency you desire.

Smoked Oyster Chowder
Serves 1-2

1 3.75-ounce can smoked oysters (or foil pouch)
1/4 cup dried potato slices
1/4 cup powdered milk
2 tablespoons dried mixed mushrooms, crumbled
2 teaspoons dried mixed vegetables
1 teaspoon dried parsley
1/2 teaspoon onion flakes
1/2 tablespoon cornstarch
1/2 tablespoon vegetable or chicken bouillon
1/8 teaspoon dried basil
1/8 teaspoon dried thyme
pinch red pepper flakes
salt and pepper to taste

At home: combine all of the ingredients in a zip locking plastic bag.

In camp: bring 1/2 to 3/4 cup water to a boil. Add soup mix and smoked oysters (no need to drain). Add water to reach desired consistency. Simmer until vegetables are reconstituted and oysters are heated through.

Chicken Corn Chowder
Serves 1-2

1 3-ounce can chicken
¼ cup powdered milk
3 tablespoons dried mushrooms
2 tablespoons dried corn
2 tablespoons dried potato slices, broken up
1 teaspoon shelf stable bacon bits
1 teaspoon dried bell pepper
1 teaspoon onion flakes
1 teaspoon dried carrots
½ tablespoon cornstarch
½ tablespoon chicken or vegetable bouillon
½ teaspoon dried chives
1/8 teaspoon dried basil
1/8 teaspoon dried thyme
Salt and pepper to taste

At home: combine everything in a zip locking plastic bag. Carry the chicken separately.

In camp: add 1 ½ to 2 cups of water to the bag. Stir and allow to sit for 5 minutes or until the vegetables are rehydrated. Add chicken (do not drain) before eating.

Salmon Chowder
Serves 1-2

¼ cup powdered milk
¼ cup dried potato slices, broken up
1 tablespoon mixed dried vegetables
1 tablespoon dried peas
½ teaspoon onion flakes
½ tablespoon corn starch
½ tablespoon chicken or vegetable bouillon powder
½ teaspoon dried basil
½ teaspoon dried thyme
1 3-ounce foil package salmon
salt and pepper to taste

At home: combine all of the dry ingredients in a zip locking plastic bag. Carry the salmon separately.

In camp: bring 1 cup of water to a boil. Add the soup mix and simmer until the vegetables are rehydrated. Add the salmon just before serving.

Cream of Shiitake and Corn Soup
Serves 1-2

Don't add the powdered ingredients when you add the shiitakes and corn. The soup will thicken before the mushrooms and corn are able to rehydrate. To make this more like chowder, pack in a small, baked at home, potato. In camp, dice the potato. Add to the cooked soup before serving and just heat through.

¼ cup dried corn
¼ cup dried shiitake mushrooms, broken up
¼ cup powdered milk
¼ cup instant mashed potato flakes
1 heaping tablespoon dried mixed vegetables
1 tablespoon vegetable bouillon
1 tablespoon dried parsley
½ teaspoon cornstarch
½ teaspoon sesame oil
1 tablespoon vegetable oil
salt and pepper to taste

At home: combine the sesame and vegetable oils in a plastic screw top container. Combine the vegetable broth powder, dried vegetables, corn, mushrooms and parsley in a zip locking plastic bag. In a second bag combine the powdered milk, instant mashed potatoes and cornstarch. Also carry take-out packages of salt and pepper.

In camp: Bring 1-¼ cups of water to a boil. Add the contents of the mushroom/corn bag. When the vegetables have rehydrated, add the contents of the milk/mashed potato bag. STIR! Season to taste with salt and pepper. Add more water if you would like a thinner soup.

Instant Vegetable Soup
Serves 1

This is a wonderfully versatile soup. The beauty of it is, you can use whatever vegetables you like. Have a different soup on every trip, based on the same recipe. Dried gourmet mushrooms are especially nice in this soup

1/3 cup dried vegetables of your choice, or a blend
2 tablespoons whole wheat couscous
½ teaspoon dried parsley
½ teaspoon dried basil
1/8 teaspoon garlic powder
1 tablespoon vegetable bouillon

At home: combine all of the ingredients in a zip locking plastic bag.

In camp: bring 2 cups of hot water to a boil. Add the soup mix, stir and remove from heat. Let stand for 5 minutes until the vegetables and couscous are reconstituted. Enjoy.

Ginger Carrot Soup
Serves 1

When testing this recipe, I tried to break up the carrots in a blender. That did not work for me. Smashing them in this way works, and it is kind of fun.

½ cup dried carrots
1 tablespoon chicken or vegetable bouillon
½ teaspoon cornstarch
½ teaspoon onion flakes
½ teaspoon ground ginger
3 tablespoons powdered milk
salt and pepper to taste

At home: place the carrots in a zip locking plastic bag. Pulverize with a meat mallet or rolling pin. Add ginger powder, onion, flakes, bouillon, cornstarch and milk powder to the bag.

In camp: bring 1 cup of water to a boil. Add carrots and simmer. Season with salt and pepper to taste.

Tomato Corn Chowder
Serves 1-2

½ cup dried corn
¼ cup powdered milk
2 tablespoons dried tomatoes
1 teaspoon butter flakes
1 teaspoon onion flakes
½ tablespoon corn starch
½ tablespoon dried parsley
¼ teaspoon oregano
¼ teaspoon thyme
salt and pepper to taste

At home: combine all of the dry ingredients in a zip locking plastic bag.

In camp: bring 1 cup of water to a boil, add the soup mix. Simmer until the corn and tomatoes have rehydrated.

Variation: to the above ingredients add a foil package of crab and ½ teaspoon Old Bay Seasoning©.

Leek and Mushroom Soup
Serves 1-2

This is a simple, but very filling soup.

½ cup shelf stable gnocchi
½ cup dried mushrooms
¼ cup instant leek soup mix (about ½ package)
3 tablespoons powdered milk
½ teaspoon parsley
salt and pepper to taste

At home: combine all the dry ingredients in a zip locking plastic bag. Carry the gnocchi in a second bag.

In camp: bring 2 cups of water to a boil. Add the gnocchi and simmer until they float to the top. Add the soup mix and simmer just until the mushrooms are rehydrated.

Vegetarian Posole
Serves 1

2 tablespoons plain TVP
2 tablespoons dried corn
2 teaspoons dried bell peppers
1 tablespoon dried tomatoes
1 teaspoon vegetable bouillon
1 teaspoon chili powder
1 teaspoon dried cilantro
½ teaspoon onion flakes
¼ teaspoon garlic powder

At home: combine everything in a zip locking plastic bag.

In camp: add enough hot water to cover, and then add more water according to your taste. Just enough to cover will give you a stew-like dish; more water will make a more soup-like dish.

Trail Tom Yum
Serves 1

1 cup rice noodles
2 tablespoons dried mushrooms (shiitakes)
1 teaspoon vegetable or chicken bouillon
1/2 teaspoon ground ginger
1/4 teaspoon dried lemongrass
1 tablespoon mixed vegetables
1/4 teaspoon garlic powder
pinch red pepper flakes (or more to taste)
2 packets True Lime© or 2 teaspoons lime juice
1 packet soy sauce

At home: package all of the dry ingredients together in a zip locking plastic bag. If you are carrying lime juice, put it in a screw top container.

In camp: bring 1 1/2 cups water to a boil. Add the soup mix. Stir and simmer until noodles are cooked.

Mushroom Tortellini
Serves 1-2

Feel free to swap out the chanterelle mushrooms for whatever variety you like.

1 cup cheese-filled mini tortellini (the dry kind)
¼ cup dried chanterelle mushrooms, broken up
1 tablespoon dried mixed vegetables
1 tablespoon chicken or vegetable bouillon
½ teaspoon dried parsley
¼ teaspoon dried thyme
¼ teaspoon onion flakes
salt and pepper to taste

At home: combine everything in a zip locking plastic bag.

In camp: bring 2 cups of water to a boil. Add the tortellini and mushroom mix. Simmer for 5 minutes or until the tortellini is tender.

Dinners

This is probably the chapter that started One Pan Wonders. My hiking buddies and I would be talking about food, regular food, and I would think "Hey! We could make that into a backpacking meal..." this happened so many times that I knew I would have to start writing (or re-writing in some cases) recipes.

Other ideas came from looking at the selection of freeze-dried dinners available. Many of the choices available can easily be assembled at home. The benefits of making your own meals are that not only do you control the ingredients; you can also control the portion size. Instead of a freeze dried salt fest, you end up with tasty meals that are customized with the ingredients YOU like. And nothing you don't. Add the vegetables and spices that you prefer. Adjust recipes for intolerances and/or allergies.

Vegetarian dinners are easily converted into larger, meat filled dinners by adding a foil package of tuna, salmon or chicken. I have not separated the vegetarian recipes out for this reason. Try swapping out different types of meats to add more variety to your meals. Try salmon in place of the shrimp in Coconut Lime Shrimp or tuna in place of the chicken in Sesame Lemon Chicken.

Chicken Tetrazzini
Serves 1-2

This recipe is a result of a challenge on a hiking forum that I frequent. Traditionally Chicken Tetrazzini is baked. This is my backpacking version.

1 5-ounce can chicken or turkey (or a foil package)
1 cup vermicelli pasta (or angel hair pasta, broken into small pieces)
¼ cup dried mushrooms
3 tablespoons powdered milk
1 tablespoon flour
1 teaspoon butter flakes
4 packets Parmesan cheese
1 teaspoon onion flakes
¼ teaspoon garlic powder
2 tablespoons dry sherry
¼ cup dry bread crumbs (optional)

At home: combine the flour, powdered milk, butter flakes and Parmesan cheese in one zip locking plastic bag. Combine the vermicelli, mushrooms, onion flakes and garlic powder in a second bag. If you are bringing the bread crumbs, place them in a third bag. Carry the dry sherry in a screw top container.

In camp: bring 1 ½ cups water to a boil. Add the pasta and cook until almost al dente. Add the milk and cheese mixture. Stir and allow to thicken. Stir in the dry sherry and top with the bread crumbs just before serving.

Sesame Lemon Chicken
Serves 1

1 3-ounce package chicken (or 3 ounce can)
1 cup angel hair pasta, broken up
¼ teaspoon ground ginger
2 tablespoons soy sauce
1 tablespoon lemon juice or 1 packet True Lemon©
½ teaspoon vegetable oil
1 tablespoon sesame seeds

At home: place the pasta in a zip locking plastic bag. In a plastic screw-top container, place the ginger, soy sauce, lemon juice, vegetable oil and sesame seeds. Carry the chicken separately.

In camp: bring 2 cups of water to a boil. Add the angel hair pasta and cook until just tender. Drain if needed. Add the chicken and sauce. Toss and serve.

Sunrise Linguine with Clams
Serves 2

I served this the first night of a 4-day Wonderland Trail trip. It was so bland the first time around. I've played with it and jazzed it up a lot!

8 ounces linguine
1 3.5-ounce package of clams
2 packets Romano or Parmesan cheese
½ teaspoon dried thyme
½ teaspoon dried parsley
¼ teaspoon garlic powder
¼ teaspoon onion powder
pinch of red pepper flakes
salt and pepper to taste
splash of white wine (optional)

At home: place all of the herbs, spices and cheese in a small zip locking plastic bag. Place the pasta in a second bag. If you are bringing the wine, place in a small screw-top bottle.

In camp: bring 3 cups of water to a boil. Cook pasta until al dente. Drain, leaving just a little water in the pan. Add the herbs, spices and cheese. Stir in the clams and their juices. Serve hot.

GoBlue Fredo
Serves 2-3

My hiking buddies and I hiked in and met our friend Mike on the last day of his solo 31-day cross country Olympic National Park trek. We brought him dinner, wine and candy. Stories and laughter flowed all night. This is what we ate.

1 6-ounce box Annie's Shells and White Cheddar
8 ounces smoked salmon (or 1 foil package of salmon or tuna)
1 cup dried corn
1 tablespoon dried basil

At home: take the pasta from the box and place in one zip locking plastic bag with the corn. In a second bag place the dried basil and cheese packet. Carry the salmon separately.

In camp: bring a pot of water to a boil. Add the pasta and cook until al dente. Drain, leaving a little bit of the hot water in the pan. Add the basil, cheese packet and salmon. Stir to combine. Serve hot.

Onion Mushroom Angel Hair Pasta
Serves 1

4 ounces angel hair pasta
¼ cup dried mushrooms
1 tablespoon vegetable bouillon
1 teaspoon butter flakes
1 teaspoon powdered milk
1 tablespoon onion flakes
½ teaspoon garlic powder
½ teaspoon dried thyme
1 tablespoon lemon zest or 1 packet True Lemon©
salt and pepper to taste

At home: combine everything in a zip locking plastic bag.

In camp: bring 1 ½ cups of water to a boil. Add the pasta. Lower the heat and simmer for about 5 minutes until the noodles are cooked and the water is absorbed. Add more water if needed.

Pesto Pistachio
Serves 1-2

4 ounces angel hair pasta, broken into thirds
¼ cup pistachios, chopped finely
1 teaspoon dried basil
½ teaspoon butter flakes
¼ teaspoon garlic powder
2 packets Parmesan cheese
2 tablespoons olive oil

At home: combine the pistachios, butter flakes, basil, garlic and cheese in a zip locking plastic bag. Put the pasta in a second bag. Carry the olive oil in a screw top container.

In camp: bring 1 cup of water to a boil. Add the pasta. Let simmer until the water is almost gone and the pasta is al dente (you want a little water left in the pan). Add the pesto mix and oil. Stir and serve.

Lemon Basil Parmesan Pasta
Serves 1-2

6 ounces spaghetti, broken up
1 teaspoon dry basil
½ teaspoon garlic powder
2 packets Parmesan cheese
1 packet True Lemon©
salt and pepper to taste
2 tablespoons olive oil

At home: combine the spaghetti, garlic powder and basil in a zip locking plastic bag. Put the packets of cheese and True Lemon© in the bag. Carry the olive oil in a screw top container.

In camp: bring 2 cups of water to a boil. Remove the cheese and True Lemon© from the bag and then add the pasta. Simmer until the water is absorbed and the pasta is cooked. Add the oil, cheese and True Lemon©. Toss and serve.

Indonesian Sesame Noodles
Serves 1

4 ounces soba or whole wheat spaghetti noodles, broken in half
1 2 ½-ounce package peanut butter (about 3 tablespoons)
2 single serving size packets of soy sauce
½ tablespoon cider vinegar
½ teaspoon sesame oil
1 single serving sugar packet
1 teaspoon onion flakes
red pepper flakes to taste

At home: put the noodles and onion flakes in a zip locking plastic bag. Put the peanut butter, soy sauce, sugar and red pepper flake packets in a second bag. Carry the cider vinegar and sesame oil in a screw top container.

In camp: bring 1 ½ cups water to a boil. Add the noodles and sugar. In the meantime, get the peanut butter and soy sauce ready to be added. Cook the noodles for about 5 minutes, or until they are almost done. Add the peanut butter and soy sauce. Shake the vinegar and oil to combine and stir into the noodles. Season with red pepper flakes before serving.

Ramen Foo Yung
Serves 1-2

A word about ramen noodles. To make this a vegetarian meal, choose a vegetarian variety of ramen. There are several available. Some are much better than others. Experiment to find one that you like.

1 3-ounce package ramen noodles (your favorite flavor)
2 fresh eggs
2 tablespoons dried (shiitake) mushrooms
2 tablespoons dried mixed vegetables, your choice
1 packet soy sauce (or to taste - optional)

At home: combine the dried mushrooms and mixed vegetables in a zip locking plastic bag. Carry the eggs in a camping/hiking egg carrier. Carry the ramen separately.

In camp: bring 2 cups water to a boil. Break up the ramen noodles and add them, with the vegetables to the water. Simmer, uncovered, until the noodles are almost done, stirring occasionally. Add the seasoning packet and soy sauce. Add eggs and stir quickly to distribute. Simmer until eggs are cooked.

Sesame Chicken & Rice with Cherries
Serves 1

1 3-ounce can chicken
1/2 cup instant rice
2 tablespoons dried cherries, cut up
1 packet True Orange©
1 teaspoon sesame seeds
1/2 teaspoon onion flakes
1/4 teaspoon ground ginger
1/4 teaspoon mustard powder
1/4 teaspoon garlic powder
salt and pepper to taste
1/2 teaspoon sesame oil
1 teaspoon rice wine vinegar

At home: combine all of the ingredients except the chicken, vinegar and oil in a zip locking plastic bag. Place the can of chicken in the bag. Combine the sesame oil and vinegar in a screw top container. Put this in the bag also.

In camp: remove the chicken, vinegar and oil from the bag. Place bag in a cozy. Add enough hot water to cover the rice. Allow to rehydrate, and then add the remaining ingredients. Stir well and enjoy.

Brimstone Chicken Wrap
Serves 1-2

This recipe is the result of a conversation on a backpacking forum. The topic was three ingredient meals. The original version did not include cheese.

1 4-ounce foil package chicken breast with barbecue sauce
1 cup instant rice
2 large flour tortillas
2 1-ounce sticks pepper Jack or cheddar cheese (optional)

At home: wrap the tortillas in foil. Place the rice in a zip locking plastic bag. Carry the cheese and chicken separately.

In camp: place the bag of rice in a cozy. Add 1 cup of hot water. Set aside for 5 minutes to rehydrate. Meanwhile shred the chicken in the package. Place half of the rice on a tortilla, top with half of the chicken and one stick of cheese. Roll and eat. Repeat with the remaining ingredients.

Chicken Cacciatore with Rice
Serves 1-2

1 3-ounce can chicken
1/2 cup instant rice
3 tablespoons mushrooms
2 tablespoons dried tomatoes
1 tablespoon tomato powder
1 tablespoon dried roasted red bell pepper (just veggies)
1/2 tablespoon shelf stable bacon or imitation bacon bits (optional)
1/2 teaspoon onion flakes
1/4 teaspoon dried basil
pinch red pepper flakes (or more - to taste)
salt and pepper to taste

At home: combine everything in a zip locking plastic bag. You can put the can of chicken in the bag as well.

In camp: remove the canned chicken from the bag. Place bag in a cozy. Add enough hot water to cover. Stir in the chicken. Let sit until rehydrated.

Coconut Lime Shrimp
Serves 1

1 3.5-ounce package shrimp
1 cup instant rice
2 tablespoons dried mushrooms, broken up
1 ½ tablespoon coconut crème powder
¼ teaspoon ground ginger
2 packets True Lime©
1 tablespoon dried mixed veggies
1 packet soy sauce
red pepper flakes to taste

At home: combine the rice, coconut powder, ginger, True Lime©, mushrooms and veggies in a zip locking plastic bag. Carry the shrimp, soy sauce and red pepper flakes separately.

In camp: bring 1 ¼ cups water to a boil. Add the rice and veggies. Simmer for 1-2 minutes until rice is almost done. Add the shrimp. Stir and allow to heat through. Serve seasoned with soy sauce and red pepper flakes.

Beef Teriyaki Rice
Serves 1

To chop up beef jerky, cut in small pieces with kitchen shears, then run through the blender or food processor.

3 tablespoons beef jerky, chopped
1/2 cup instant rice
1 tablespoon dried vegetables
1/2 teaspoon brown sugar
1-2 tablespoons soy sauce or packets
1/4 teaspoon powdered ginger
pinch red pepper flakes (or more, to taste)

At home: combine everything except the soy sauce in a zip locking plastic bag.

In camp: bring 1 cup of water to a boil. Add rice mixture and summer until rice is tender. Add soy sauce and red pepper flakes to taste.

Curried Beef and Rice with Peaches
Serves 1

1/3 cup instant rice
2 tablespoons dried peaches, chopped
1 tablespoon beef jerky, shredded
1 packet True Lemon©
½ teaspoon ground cinnamon
½ teaspoon sugar
¼ teaspoon curry powder
1/8 teaspoon ground ginger
salt and pepper to taste

At home: combine everything in a zip locking plastic bag.

In camp: place bag in a cozy. Add enough water to cover the rice mixture; about ½ cup. Let stand for 5 minutes, or until the rice is tender. Stir well to distribute the spices before eating.

Variation: try golden raisins or dried apricots in place of the dried peaches.

Pineapple Sesame Rice
Serves 1-2

1 cup instant rice
¼ cup dried pineapple, finely chopped
2 tablespoons soy sauce (or 1-2 packets)
1 teaspoon sesame oil
1 packet honey
1 teaspoon dried onion flakes
¼ teaspoon garlic powder
1 tablespoon sesame seeds, carried separately
red pepper flakes to taste

At home: combine the rice, pineapple, onion and garlic in a zip locking plastic bag. Carry the soy sauce and sesame oil in a screw top container. Carry the sesame seeds, honey and red pepper flakes separately.

In camp: bring 1 ¼ cups of water to a boil. Add rice mix. Simmer for 1-2 minutes or until rice is tender and cooked. Stir in sesame oil, soy sauce and honey. Season with red pepper flakes. Serve topped with sesame seeds.

Trailhead Ropa Vieja
Serves 1

This recipe is adapted from my friend Lynn's recipe. Her version calls for a dehydrator.

1 cup instant rice
1/4 cup beef jerky, shredded
2 tablespoons tomato powder
2 tablespoons onion flakes
1 teaspoon beef bouillon
1 teaspoon dried parsley
½ teaspoon dried oregano
½ teaspoon dried basil
¼ teaspoon dried red pepper flakes (or more to taste)
salt and pepper to taste

At home: combine all of the ingredients in zip locking plastic bag.

In camp: add one cup hot water, stir and place in a cozy for five minutes.

Unstuffed Peppers
Serves 1

1/3 cup instant rice
3 tablespoons dried bell peppers
1 tablespoon cilantro
1 tablespoon tomato powder
1 tablespoon sun dried tomatoes, chopped
1 tablespoon dried mixed vegetables
1/2 teaspoon dried oregano
1/2 teaspoon vegetable bouillon
1/4 teaspoon garlic powder

At home: combine everything in a zip locking bag

In camp: add enough hot water to cover. Stir and place in a cozy. Allow to stand for 5 minutes or until the vegetables are rehydrated. Stir well and eat.

Five Spice Mushroom Rice
Serves 1

You can add a package of tofu or chicken to this to make it a more substantial meal.

1/2 cup instant rice
¼ cup dried mushrooms, broken up
¼ teaspoon five spice powder
¼ teaspoon onion flakes
pinch of sugar
salt and pepper to taste

At home: combine everything in a zip locking plastic bag.

In camp: bring 1 cup of water to a boil. Add the contents of the bag. Simmer for 1-2 minutes or until the rice is tender and the water is absorbed.

Curried Rice
Serves 1. Serves 2 if you add a foil pack of chicken or tofu.

1 cup instant rice
½ tablespoon curry powder
1 tablespoon dried onion flakes
¼ tablespoon sugar
½ tablespoon chicken or vegetable bouillon
½ teaspoon garlic powder
1/8 teaspoon ground turmeric
salt to taste
3 tablespoons cashews, chopped (optional)

At home: combine everything in a zip locking plastic bag.
If you are bringing a foil pack of chicken, carry that separately.

In camp: bring 1 cup of water to a boil. Add rice mix and simmer
for about 1-2 minutes or until the rice is tender.
Serve topped with chopped cashews.

Salmon Hazelnut Couscous
Serves 1

1 3-ounce package salmon
1/3 cup couscous
1/4 cup hazelnuts, chopped
1 tablespoon dried parsley
1/4 teaspoon garlic powder
2 packets True Lemon©
salt and pepper to taste
olive oil to taste

At home: combine everything except the salmon and olive oil in a zip locking plastic bag. Carry the olive oil in a screw top container and the salmon separately.

In camp: add just enough water to the couscous to cover and place in a cozy. Tuck the pouch of salmon in the cozy to warm. Set aside for 5-10 minutes. Fluff the couscous and add the salmon. Add salt, pepper and olive oil to taste.

Sesame Ginger Couscous
Serves 1

1/3 cup couscous
1 tablespoon dried carrots
1 tablespoon dried shiitake mushrooms
1/2 teaspoon onion flakes
1/4 teaspoon ground ginger
1/2 teaspoon sesame oil
1 teaspoon soy sauce

At home: combine the sesame oil and soy sauce in a screw top container. Combine the remaining ingredients in zip locking plastic bag.

In camp: add enough hot water to cover. Stir and let stand for 5 minutes. Eat!

Eagle's Roost Ginger Curry Couscous
Serves 2-3

We had this for dinner on the third day of a four day Wonderland Trail trip. This makes a lot! I fed myself and shared the leftovers with two other hikers. Coconut crème powder would be a nice addition. If you like fruit in this sort of thing, diced, dried apricots or golden raisins are excellent.

2 cups couscous
2 teaspoons curry powder
2 teaspoons ground ginger
¾ cup cashews, chopped
1 ½ cups dried vegetables

At home: in a zip locking plastic bag, combine the couscous, curry powder, ginger and vegetables. Place the cashews in a separate bag.

In camp: bring 4 cups of water to a boil. Add to couscous to the water, cover and remove from heat. Let stand for 5-10 minutes until the couscous is cooked. Fluff and top with the cashews before serving.

Lemon Pistachio Couscous
Serves 1

½ cup couscous
1 teaspoon chicken or vegetable bouillon
1 teaspoon lemon zest
1 tablespoons pistachios, shelled and chopped
salt and pepper to taste

At home: combine the couscous and lemon zest in a zip locking plastic bag. Carry pistachios separately.

In camp: bring 1 cup of water to a boil. Add couscous. Stir and remove from heat. Let stand for about 5 minutes, or until the water is absorbed. Stir in the pistachios, fluff the couscous and eat.

Pesto Potatoes with Salmon
Serves 1

1/2 cup dried potato slices
1 3-ounce package of salmon
2 tablespoons dried mixed vegetables
1 tablespoon dry pesto sauce (from packet)
1 tablespoon powdered milk
1/2 teaspoon butter powder
1-2 packets Parmesan cheese
salt and pepper to taste

At home: combine everything except the salmon and cheese in a zip locking plastic bag. Carry the salmon and Parmesan separately.

In camp: bring 1 cup of water to a boil. Add the potatoes and vegetables. When the potatoes are tender, add the salmon. Serve topped with Parmesan cheese.

Garlic Wasabi Mashed Potatoes
Serves 1-2

I like the Idahoan© brand mashed potatoes. No need to re-bag!
Wasabi powder is available in the Asian foods section of larger supermarkets, in Asian grocery stores and online.

1 4-ounce package butter-flavored instant mashed potatoes
2 tablespoons wasabi powder
2 tablespoons powdered milk
1 tablespoon garlic powder
½ teaspoon black pepper

At home: combine the powdered milk, garlic, wasabi powder and pepper in a zip locking plastic bag. Carry the mashed potatoes separately, or add them to the bag.

In camp: bring 2 cups of water to a boil. Add everything, stirring to break up any lumps. Remove from heat and continue stirring until thickened.

Cider Glazed Sweet Potatoes with Cranberries
Serves 1

Sweet potatoes and yams can be used interchangeably. I like yams for their color and sweetness. You could also add mini marshmallows if you want dinner to be extra sweet.

1 sweet potato, baked at home
½ cup dried cranberries
¼ cup chopped pecans or walnuts
1 1-ounce packet instant hot apple cider mix
2 tablespoons brown sugar
1 single serving packet butter

At home: bake the sweet potato. Let cool. Place in a zip locking plastic bag. In a second bag, carry the apple cider mix, brown sugar and cranberries. Carry the butter packet and nuts separately.

In camp: bring ½ to 3/4 cup water to a simmer (just enough to dissolve the sugar and drink mix). Add the sweet potatoes and heat through. Serve topped with the chopped nuts.

Chicken with Bulgur
Serves 1

1 3-ounce can chicken
1/4 cup bulgur
1 tablespoon golden raisins
1 tablespoon dried mixed veggies
1/2 teaspoon onion flakes
1/2 teaspoon parsley flakes
1/4 teaspoon chicken bouillon
1/4 teaspoon ground coriander
1/4 teaspoon cinnamon
1/8 teaspoon allspice

At home: combine everything except the chicken in a zip locking plastic bag. You can add the can of chicken to the bag.

In camp: remove the can of chicken from the bag. Place bag in a cozy. Add enough hot water to cover. Stir and let stand for 5 minutes. Stir in the chicken and enjoy.

Bulgur and Rice Mushroom Pilaf
Serves 1-2

1/4 cup bulgur
1/4 cup instant rice
3 tablespoons dried mushrooms
1 teaspoons vegetable bouillon
1 packet True Lemon©
1/4 teaspoon dried thyme
1/4 teaspoon onion flakes
1/4 teaspoon dried parsley

At home: combine everything in a zip locking plastic bag.

In camp: place bag in a cozy. Add enough hot water to cover. Stir. The bulgur will sink to the bottom. Let stand for 5 minutes, or until the rice and bulgur are tender. Stir again before eating.

Dungeness Blue Gnocchi
Serves 2

8 ounces shelf stable gnocchi
1/4 cup blue cheese, crumbled
2 tablespoons powdered milk
1 tablespoon shelf stable bacon
2 packets Parmesan or Romano cheese
1 tablespoon olive oil

At home: combine the cheese, bacon and powdered milk in a small plastic container with a lid. Carry the gnocchi in a zip locking plastic bag and the olive oil in a screw top container.

In camp: bring water to a boil Add the gnocchi. When the gnocchi floats to the top; drain, leaving about a tablespoon of water in the pan. Add the blue cheese mixture and olive oil. Stir well. Enjoy.

Alice Lake Alfredo Gnocchi
Serves 1

Bring a hunk of bread to mop up the extra sauce.

6 ounces (about 1/3 package) shelf stable gnocchi
2 tablespoons dry alfredo sauce (about ½ package)
¼ cup powdered milk
1 teaspoon dried bell pepper
½ teaspoon dried rosemary, crumbled
1/8 teaspoon garlic powder (more or less, depending on the brand of alfredo
sauce you use)
1-2 tablespoons olive oil (optional)
Salt and pepper to taste

At home: combine all of the dry ingredients, except the gnocchi in a zip locking
plastic bag. Place the gnocchi and the bag of dry ingredients in a second bag.
Carry the olive oil in a screw top container.

In camp: bring water to a boil. Add the gnocchi and simmer until they float to the
top. Drain all except about a cup of water from the pan. The gnocchi will be
barely swimming in water. Add the dry ingredients. Stir until sauce is thickened.
Add oil if desired.

Gnocchi with Sage Butter Parmesan and Bacon
Serves 2

Comfort food heaven! Shelf stable gnocchi can be found at Trader Joe's and well
stocked supermarkets.

1 8-ounce package prepared gnocchi
½ cup Parmesan cheese, shredded
3 tablespoons shelf stable bacon crumbles
2 individual packages butter
1 teaspoon dried sage
1 teaspoon garlic powder
¼ teaspoon black pepper

At home: combine the Parmesan cheese, sage, garlic powder and black pepper in
a zip-locking plastic bag. Carry the bacon in a second bag. You can re-package the
gnocchi into a baggie if you'd like to save room in your pack.

In camp: bring a pan of water to a boil. Add the gnocchi and cook for about 2
minutes. The gnocchi will float to the surface when it is done. Drain. Add the
Parmesan and spices. Stir. Add the bacon and stir again before serving.

Cherry Chicken Stuffing
Serves 1-2

My husband LOVES this. High praise indeed - he's Mr. Picky-Pants.

1 6-ounce box stuffing mix with seasonings (chicken flavor Stove Top)
1 3-ounce can chicken
2 tablespoons dried cherries, cut up

At home: put the stuffing in a zip locking plastic bag and the cherries in a second bag. Carry the chicken separately.

In camp: bring 1 1/2 cups of water to a boil. Add the stuffing. Allow to rehydrate, and then stir in the chicken (with juices) and the dried cherries. Stir and eat!

Kendall Katwalk Chicken and Dumplings
Serves 2

I made this up to impress a certain someone on a one-nighter Pacific Crest Trail trip. It started off as a joke, but the recipe worked! My hiking buddies were drooling in my pan. That night we watched the full moon rise, lighting up the mountains around us. Simply amazing. That special someone is now my husband.

1 7-ounce foil package chicken
2 1/4 cups Bisquick® mix
1 tablespoon chicken bouillon
1 tablespoon dried vegetable flakes
1 tablespoon dried onion flakes
1 teaspoon dried parsley
1/2 teaspoon celery salt
1/4 teaspoon black pepper
1/4 teaspoon dried thyme

At home: put the Bisquick® and parsley in a zip locking plastic bag. In a second bag put the remaining ingredients. Carry the chicken pouch separately.

In camp: bring 3 cups of water to a boil, add the broth/veggie mix. Reduce heat and keep simmering. Add the chicken. Meanwhile, make the dumplings by adding 2/3 cup of water to the bag of Bisquick®. Zip shut and squish to combine well. Snip off a corner off the bag and squeeze out dumplings. Let them simmer, covered, for a couple of minutes or until they puff up and float to the top.

Sheep Lake Mush
Serves 1

¼ cup cornmeal
1 tablespoon dried vegetables
2 packets of Parmesan or Romano cheese
1 tablespoon dried mushrooms, broken up
1 tablespoon powdered milk
1 teaspoon butter powder
¼ teaspoon dried thyme
salt and pepper to taste.

At home: combine everything except the cheese in a zip locking plastic bag. Carry the cheese separately.

In camp: bring 1 cup of water to a boil. Add the cornmeal mixture and stir. Simmer until thickened and serve.

Swimming Bear Lake Rama
Serves 2

8 ounces extra firm tofu (not the kind swimming in water)
1 packet of peanut sauce mix (from a 3.5 ounce package – contains 2 packets)
3 tablespoons coconut crème powder
3 ounces fresh spinach (about ½ bag)
2 tablespoons vegetable or peanut oil

At home: put the spinach in a zip locking plastic bag. Put the coconut crème powder and peanut sauce mix in a second bag. Carry the oil in a screw top container.

In camp: heat the oil in your pan. Cut the tofu into ¾ inch cubes. Fry in the oil until golden. Add 8 ounces water. Bring to a boil. Add the peanut sauce and coconut crème powder. Stir well. Reduce heat and simmer for 1 minute. Add the spinach, stir and serve immediately.

Desserts

This was a hard chapter to write. Beyond puddings, cheesecakes and cobblers, what else can you do in the backcountry for dessert? Refrigeration, aside from an icy river or winter temperatures, is non-existent. Fresh fruit is heavy, and many types don't pack well. Fresh apples pack beautifully, cut or not, but bananas and apricots (for example) can turn into a slimy mess.

For one or two nights, snack-packs of pudding and other luxuries are easily carried in. It is easy to dress up an instant cheesecake or mousse mix to make a fancy backcountry dessert. I like taking the store-bought packages and fixing them up with my own favorite flavorings and ingredients.

The desserts on the following pages rely on existing mixes from the grocery store, as well as dried fruits and powdered products such as milk and coconut crème powder. I've used spices and spirits to make them a little more interesting.

Sugar and fat add extra needed calories to keep you going and warm. Plus it is really satisfying to follow up a delicious dinner with a decadent dessert. As an added bonus, it is fun to surprise your hiking partners with a treat at the end of a long day of hiking.

Hint: to help puddings, mousse, and cheesecakes to set up, the night before your trip, put a filled water bottle in the freezer. Let it freeze overnight (don't forget it!). Pack it in the center of your pack. You will have icy cold water when it is time to make dessert.

Lemon Ginger Pudding
Serves 2-4

Look for the Nido™ brand of instant milk. It makes the best puddings. You won't even know it is instant! It is up to you how finely you want your gingersnaps crushed. If you want bits of crunch in your pudding, leave some big chunks.

Note: do NOT add the lemonade powder to the lemon pudding or it won't set up. It does, however make a very nice lemon sauce.

1 3-ounce box instant lemon pudding
2/3 cup powdered milk
2 tablespoons sweetened instant lemonade powder
1 tablespoon powdered ginger (optional)
10 gingersnaps, crushed
2 tablespoons candied ginger, chopped finely

At home: combine the lemon pudding and powdered milk in a zip locking plastic bag. In a second bag place the gingersnaps. The easiest way I've found to crush them is to put them in the bag, then whack them with a rolling pin or meat tenderizer. And it's fun! Add the chopped candied ginger, lemonade powder and powdered ginger to the gingersnaps and toss to combine.

In camp: Mix 2 cups of water into the pudding mix. When well mixed, top with the gingersnaps and candied ginger and serve.

Vanilla Pudding with Brandied Cherries
Serves 2-4

This one is for grown-ups only!

1 3-ounce box instant vanilla pudding
2/3 cup powdered milk
2 tablespoons dried cherries, chopped finely
2 tablespoons brandy

At home: combine the pudding and powdered milk in a zip locking plastic bag. Put the brandy in a plastic screw top container. Carry the cherries separately.

In camp: in a cup or bowl, combine the dried cherries and brandy. Set aside to soak. Add 2 cups of water to the pudding mix. Mix well and set in a cold stream or snow to set up. Top the pudding with the brandy-soaked cherries after the pudding has set.

Double Coconut Pudding
Serves 2-4 but can be divided in half

1 3-ounce package instant coconut pudding
1/3 cup coconut crème powder
1/3 cup powdered milk
3 tablespoons dried mangoes, chopped finely
2 tablespoons shredded coconut, toasted (optional)

At home: combine everything in a zip locking plastic bag.

In camp: add 2 cups of water to the pudding mix. Stir well and set aside until firm. (If you've divided the mix in half, adjust water accordingly.)

Vanilla Spice Rice Pudding
Serves 2

1/2 cup instant rice
1/4 cup French vanilla instant pudding (about half of a 3-ounce box)
2 tablespoons powdered milk
1/2 teaspoon ground cinnamon
1/4 teaspoon ground nutmeg

At home: place the rice in a zip locking plastic bag. Put the rest of the ingredients in a second zip locking plastic bag.

In camp: add 1 cup of hot water to the rice. Stir and let stand for about a minute, or until the rice is tender. It will be runny, don't worry. Add the pudding mix. Stir well to combine. Eat warm or allow to cool.

Arroz con Leche
Serves 1

This makes a wonderful breakfast too! If you want a sweeter end product, add a little brown sugar or honey to the final dish.

1/2 cup instant rice
3 tablespoons powdered milk
2 tablespoons raisins
1 teaspoon ground cinnamon
pinch nutmeg

At home: combine everything in a zip locking plastic bag.

In camp: place the bag in a cozy and add just enough hot water to cover the rice. Seal the bag and the cozy and let sit for 5 minutes. Stir well before eating. Serve warm.

Mangoes in Coconut Milk
Serves 1-2

This is a great dessert to serve after a spicy dinner.

¼ cup dried mangoes, diced
2 tablespoons coconut crème powder
2 tablespoons instant rice

At home: combine the coconut crème powder and rice in a zip locking plastic bag. Place the mangoes in a second bag.

In camp: bring 8 ounces of water to a boil. Add mangoes. Turn off heat and let stand for 2-3 minutes, or until the mangoes are softened. Add the coconut crème powder and rice. Stir and let stand until rice is tender. Serve warm.

Layered Caramel Apple Cheesecake
Serves 4

1 11.1-ounce package instant cheesecake mix
1/2 cup powdered milk
1/2 cup dried apples, diced
1 1-ounce packet instant hot apple cider
1 2-ounce container caramel dip
1 teaspoon cinnamon
1/2 teaspoon nutmeg
2 tablespoons brown sugar
1/4 cup chopped pecans (optional)

At home: combine cheesecake mix, powdered milk and apple cider mix in a zip locking plastic bag. Label this bag "Add 1 1/2 cups water". In a second bag, combine spices and dried apples. You can put the caramel dip in this bag for storage. In a third bag, combine the crust mix, sugar and optional pecans. (Tip: You might want to divide the crust mix in half. It does make a lot of topping and can end up with your "crust" being too powdery.)

In camp: remove caramel dip from the apple bag and set aside. Add enough water to the apples to cover. Set them aside to rehydrate. Combine the cheesecake mix and 1 ½ cups water in your cooking pan. Stir well, breaking up any lumps. Allow to sit for a minute or two to begin setting up. Place in a snow bank or cold stream if necessary. Spoon or pour the caramel dip on top of the cheesecake, distributing as evenly as possible. When the apples are rehydrated, top the caramel layer with them. Do not include any extra liquid from the bag. Top the apple layer with the crust. Set aside until firm.

Butter Rum Cheesecake
Serves 4

1 11.1-ounce package instant cheesecake mix
1/2 cup powdered milk
¼ cup butterscotch chips, chopped coarsely
1 mini bottle spiced rum
1 tablespoon brown sugar
1 teaspoon cinnamon
¼ teaspoon nutmeg
½ teaspoon allspice

At home: place the cheesecake part of the mix and the powdered milk in a zip locking plastic bag. Place ½ half of the crust mix in a second zip locking bag with the spices, butterscotch chips and brown sugar. (Use the other half of the crust mix for something else.)

In camp: combine the cheesecake mix, rum and about 1 ¼ cups water in your pan. Stir until there are no more lumps. Set aside, in a cold stream or snow bank if necessary. When beginning to set up, top with crust mix. Serve once the cheesecake has completely set.

Grand Marnier® Chocolate Mousse
Serves 2-4

This dessert is extremely rich. Don't try it if you don't like Grand Marnier®!

1 4.2-ounce box instant chocolate mousse mix
1/3 cup powdered milk
1 mini bottle Grand Marnier®
2 tablespoons mini chocolate chips

At home: combine chocolate mousse mix and powdered milk in a zip locking plastic bag. Carry the chocolate chips in a snack sized bag and the Grand Marnier® separately.

In camp: add Grand Marnier® and enough water to total 1 cup liquid (about ¾ cup water – use less liquor for a milder flavor). Stir well and set aside until firmed up. Serve topped with chocolate ships.

Caramel Macadamia Tarts
Serves 2

Half of a pudding snack pack fits perfectly on one tart shell. The creaminess of the pudding balances out the sweetness of the caramel. I had originally thought about topping this with chocolate syrup or mini chocolate chips, but I think that would be overkill. Chocolate caramel dip would rock though!

2 mini graham cracker tart shells (they come in a box of 6)
1 snack-pack of vanilla pudding cup
1 2-ounce container caramel apple dip
1/4 cup macadamia nuts, chopped

At home: put the nuts in a zip locking plastic bag. Carefully pack the tart shells in a second bag. Carry the caramel and pudding separately.

In camp: assemble your tarts. First coat the bottom of each tart shell with half of the caramel. Top this with half of the macadamia nuts. Next, top with half of the vanilla pudding. Eat and enjoy! (Don't forget to pack out the foil tart pan and other containers.)

Chocolate Peanut Butter Pies
Serves 2

2 mini graham cracker tart shells (they come in a box of 6)
1 snack-pack of chocolate pudding cup
4 tablespoons peanut butter
2 tablespoons mini chocolate chips

At home: put the chocolate chips in a snack sized zip locking plastic bag. Carry the pudding and tart shells separately. Carry the peanut butter in a small screw top container.

In camp: spread half of the peanut butter on each of the tart shells. Top with half of the pudding, then half of the chocolate chips.

Strawberry Vanilla Tarts
Serves 2

2 tart shells
1 snack pack vanilla pudding cup
1 2-ounce package strawberry shortcake glaze

At home: package everything separately.

In camp: spread half of the shortcake glaze on each of the tart shells. Top with half of the pudding.

Trail Tiramisu
Serves 2

2 tablespoons instant coffee
1/2 teaspoon ground cinnamon
12 vanilla wafers
2 snack packs vanilla pudding cups

At home: put the instant coffee and cinnamon in a small screw top container. Package the vanilla wafers in a zip locking plastic bag. Carry the pudding separately.

In camp: add 3-4 tablespoons water to the coffee and cinnamon. Shake well to combine. Put about ¼ of the vanilla wafers in a cup or bowl. Break them up a little if they aren't already. Pour ¼ of the coffee over. Top with half of one of the pudding cups. Top with more of the vanilla wafers and coffee. Top with the other half of the pudding cup. Repeat for the second serving.

Stewed Apples with Gingerbread Dumplings
Serves 1-2

½ cup dried apples, chopped
¼ cup gingerbread cake/cookie mix
3 tablespoons Bisquick™
1 tablespoon brown sugar
½ teaspoon butter powder
¼ teaspoon ground cinnamon
pinch nutmeg

At home: combine the apples, brown sugar, butter powder, cinnamon and nutmeg in a zip locking plastic bag. In a second bag, combine the gingerbread cake mix and Bisquick™.

In camp: add apples to 1 cup of hot water. Simmer until tender, adding more water if necessary. Meanwhile, add ¼ cup water to the dumpling mix. Squish the bag until thoroughly combined. Cut off a corner of the bag and drop small dumplings into the simmering apples. Simmer until dumplings are puffed up and cooked through. You may need to flip them to get the dumplings cooked on all sides. It will depend on how much water is left in your pan.

Sopapillas
Serves 2

You will need to bring some paper towels or napkins to drain these on.

2 8-inch flour tortillas
1 teaspoon cinnamon
1 tablespoon sugar
¼ cup vegetable oil

At home: combine the cinnamon and sugar in a snack sized zip locking plastic bag. Carry the oil in a screw top container. Wrap the tortillas in foil or plastic wrap.

In camp: heat oil in your pan. Meanwhile cut the tortillas into fourths. Fry the tortillas until very lightly golden brown. Drain on paper towels. Sprinkle with cinnamon-sugar and serve warm

Variation 1: in place of the cinnamon-sugar mixture, try 1 teaspoon five-spice powder and 1 tablespoon sugar.

Variation 2: add 2 packets True Orange© to the cinnamon-sugar mixture.

Variation 3: omit the cinnamon-sugar mixture and serve with your favorite jam or jelly (in single serving packets)

Nutella with Graham Crackers
Serves 1

4 tablespoons Nutella™
1 cup graham cracker sticks (or regular graham crackers)

At home: put the Nutella™ in a plastic container with a lid. Put the graham crackers in a zip locking plastic bag. You can put the plastic container in the bag as well.

In camp: dip and eat!

Beverages

Someone once said, "hydrate or die." Truer words have yet to be spoken. Unfortunately the days of drinking straight from rivers and streams is gone. Water treatment is crucial to prevent giardia and other ailments. Iodine and chlorine are commonly used to treat water in the backcountry. Neither tastes very good. I like to use a variety of mixes to disguise the taste of chemically treated water.

Doing this also helps me to remember to drink enough fluids. If it tastes good, I will most likely drink more of it. Being dehydrated is no fun. I start tripping over my feet when I haven't had enough water while hiking. When that starts to happen, I know it is time for a break and a good long drink of something cool. I will never forget the blue Gatorade we had on the Wonderland Trail. Not my favorite flavor, but it probably saved me that day.

For me, coffee in the morning is non-negotiable. I have to have it! On the trail is no place to get a caffeine headache. It is easy to put together a mix at home so that all you have to do in camp is add hot water. Alternately, a handful of chocolate covered espresso beans are a quick remedy for a stove-free caffeine fix.

After or before dinner cocktails are a treat in camp. I enjoy sipping a boozy beverage after dinner, while watching the sun set in the backcountry. Fresh, clean snow is a great addition to Trailgaritas. However, backpacking is not the time or place to get sloppy drunk and out of control. Drink responsibly, but enjoy the cocktail recipes.

Maple Cinnamon Latte
Serves 1

1 teaspoon instant coffee
1 teaspoon non-dairy creamer
¼ teaspoon ground cinnamon
1 tablespoon maple syrup

At home: combine all of the dry ingredients in a zip locking plastic bag. Carry the maple syrup in a screw top container. Or bring along take out packages of maple syrup.

In camp: bring 1 cup of water to a boil. Add the coffee and then the syrup. Stir well and enjoy.

French Vanilla Coffee Mix
Makes about 2 cups

This is fantastic. Very creamy.

2/3 cup instant coffee
2/3 cup sugar
½ cup instant dry milk powder
½ cup powdered coffee creamer
1 3-ounce package instant vanilla pudding mix

At home: mix all of the ingredients together and store in a zip locking plastic bag.

In camp: combine 3-4 tablespoons of mix with 8 ounces hot water.

Toffee Coffee
Makes about 2 cups

2/3 cup instant coffee
2/3 cup sugar
½ cup powdered milk
½ cup powdered coffee creamer
1 3-ounce package instant butterscotch pudding

At home: combine all of the ingredients in an air tight container. Package as much as you would like to take on the trail in a zip locking plastic bag.

In camp: bring 1 cup of water to a boil. Add 3-4 tablespoons of mix, depending on how strong you would like your coffee. Stir and enjoy!

Cinnamon Orange Coffee
Makes 1 1/2 cups

1/2 cup instant coffee crystals
1/2 cup granulated sugar
1/2 cup powdered milk
1 tablespoon nondairy creamer
1 teaspoon cinnamon
1 packet True Orange© or 1 teaspoon orange zest (dry)

At home: combine all of the ingredients together and store in zip locking plastic bag.

In camp: combine 3 teaspoons of mix with 8 ounces of hot water.

Citrus Tea
Makes 1 cup mix

1/3 cup unsweetened iced tea powder
1/3 cup orange flavored powdered drink mix
1/3 cup powdered lemonade mix

At home: combine all of the powders together. Store in an airtight container. Package as much mix as you'd like to bring on the trail in a zip locking plastic bag.

In camp: add about 2 tablespoons of mix to 8 ounces hot or cold water. Stir well and drink.

Spicy Fruit Iced Tea
Makes 1 ½ cups mix

½ cup unsweetened instant iced tea powder
1/3 cup powdered lemonade mix
1/3 cup orange flavored powdered drink mix
1/3 cup sweetened cherry flavored powdered drink mix
½ teaspoon ground cinnamon
1/8 teaspoon nutmeg
pinch cloves

At home: combine all of the powders together. Store in an airtight container. Package as much mix as you'd like to bring on the trail in a zip locking plastic bag.

In camp: add about 1 tablespoon of mix to 8 ounces cold water. Stir well and drink.

Creamy Orange Chai
Makes about 1 cup mix

½ cup orange flavored powdered drink mix
¼ cup instant chai tea mix
3 tablespoons powdered milk

At home: combine all of the powders together. Store in an airtight container. Package as much mix as you'd like to bring on the trail in a zip locking plastic bag.

In camp: add about 2-3 tablespoons of mix to 8 ounces hot or cold water. Stir well and drink.

Coconut Hot Chocolate
Serves 1

1 1-ounce packet instant hot chocolate
2 tablespoons coconut creme powder

At home: combine the hot chocolate and coconut creme powder in a zip locking plastic bag.

In camp: bring 8 ounces hot water to a boil. Add hot chocolate mix and enjoy.

Peppermint Mocha Mix
Makes about 1/2 cup

1/2 cup powdered milk
2 tablespoons cocoa powder
2 tablespoons sugar
1 tablespoon instant coffee
4 peppermint (starlite) candies

At home: place the candies in a plastic bag and crush them (I use a meat mallet) into a powder. Combine everything in a zip locking plastic bag.

In camp: add 1-2 tablespoons mix to 8 ounces of hot water. Stir well and enjoy.

Extra Spicy Hot Apple Cider
Serves 1-2

I can't take credit for this one. My friend, Jin, gave me this idea. Wow! If you like hot apple cider you have to try this! This makes an extra spicy hot apple cider. Oh so yummy!! It is a perfect hot drink for winter trips.

1 1-ounce packet hot apple cider
1 1-ounce packet instant Chai tea mix (Oregon Chai©)

At home: package the instant drink mixes to carry on the trail; no need to repackage them.

In camp: add the contents of both packages to 8-16 ounces hot water, depending on how strong you would like your drink. Stir well and enjoy.

Caramel Apple Cider
Serves 1

1 1-ounce packet instant hot apple cider mix
1 2-ounce container caramel apple dip

At home: pack the cider mix and caramel apple dip separately.

In camp: add 8 ounces hot water to your cup. Add the cider mix and caramel dip.

Hint: do NOT put the caramel in first or you will have a sticky mess.

Ginger Lemonade
1 big serving – very refreshing!

4 tablespoons powdered lemonade mix
½ teaspoon ground ginger

At home: combine the ingredients in a zip locking plastic bag.

In camp/on the trail: add the mix to 32 ounces of water. Shake well.

Hot Ginger Lemonade
Serves 1

This weighs almost nothing and is wonderful for cold nights on the trail. Multiply as needed.

2 packets True Lemon©
1 single serving size packet honey
½ teaspoon powdered ginger

At home: put the powdered ginger in a small zip locking plastic bag. Carry the True Lemon© and honey packets separately.

In camp: combine everything with 8 ounces of hot water. Stir and enjoy!

Cherry LimeAde
Serves 1-2

2 tablespoons sweetened cherry flavored drink mix
4 packets of True Lime©

At home: combine the powders together. Store in an airtight container or small zip locking plastic bag. Small, plastic baby food jars are perfect for this.

In camp: add about 1 tablespoon of mix to 8 ounces of water. Adjust strength to your liking by adding more mix or more water.

Trailgaritas
serves 1-2

4 packets True Lime©
2 tablespoons powdered lemonade mix
1 mini bottle tequila

At home: combine the True Lime© and lemonade mix in a zip locking plastic bag or screw top container. Carry the tequila separately.

In camp: add the powdered mix to 12 ounces cold water. Stir well, then add the tequila. Even better if you have clean snow to add to the mix!

Golden Apple Cider
Serves 1-2

1-2 1-ounce packets instant hot apple cider (If you want a strong cinnamon flavor, bring 1 packet. If you want a milder drink, bring 2.)
1 mini bottle Goldschläger

At home: package the cider and Goldschläger separately.

In camp: prepare apple cider according to package directions. Add Goldschläger to hot cider and serve hot.

Almond Hot Chocolate
Serves 2

2 1-ounce packets instant hot chocolate
1 mini bottle amaretto

At home: package the hot chocolate and amaretto separately.

In camp: prepare the hot chocolate to package directions. Add amaretto and serve hot.

Peppy Hot Chocolate
Serves 1

1 1-ounce packet instant hot chocolate
1 mini bottle peppermint schnapps

At home: package the hot chocolate and peppermint schnapps separately.

In camp: prepare the hot chocolate to package directions. Add peppermint schnapps and serve hot.

Sample Menus

Menu #1 - No Cook 2 Day Trip

Breakfast: at home
Lunch: Apple Bean Salad
Dinner: Smokey Crackers, Cheery Cherry Chicken Wrap

Breakfast: Cold Cereal with Powdered Milk
Lunch: Hula Wrap
Dinner: at home

Menu #2 - Leisurely 2 Day Trip

Breakfast: at home
Lunch: Ranch Chicken Wrap
Snack: Split Pea Dip, crackers
Dinner: Pineapple Sesame Rice
Dessert: Double Coconut Pudding

Breakfast: Peanut Butter Chocolate Chip Pancakes
Lunch: Chicken Salad with Corn
Dinner: at home

Menu#3 – Vegetarian 2 Day Trip

Breakfast: at home
Lunch: Cuban Burritos, cheese
Snack: Lodge Lake Tapenade, crackers
Dinner: Instant Minestrone, Pesto Pistachio
Dessert: Caramel Macadamia Tarts

Breakfast: Blueberry Bulgur
Lunch: Apple Cheddar Wrap
Snack: Wasabi Almonds, dried fruit
Dinner: at home

Menu #4 – Vegetarian 2 Day Trip (#2)

Breakfast: at home
Lunch: Vegan Instant Lunch
Snack: dried fruit, nuts
Dinner: Vegetarian Posole, Five Spice Mushroom Rice
Dessert: Lemon Ginger Pudding

Breakfast: Green & Gold Tofu Scramble
Lunch: Black Bean Wrap
Dinner: at home

Menu #5 – Fall/Winter Comfort Food – 2 Day Trip

Breakfast: at home
Lunch: White Bean Tuna Salad
Snack: dried fruit, chocolate, Wasabi Almonds
Dinner: Dungeness Blue Gnocchi
Dessert: Stewed Apples with Gingerbread Dumplings

Breakfast: Peaches and Cream Oatmeal
Lunch: Ford Wraps
Dinner: at home

Menu #6 – Spring Rain – 2 Day Trip

Breakfast: at home
Lunch: Sun Dried Tomato and White Bean Salad
Snack: crackers, cheese, Owyhigh Mix
Dinner: Salmon Chowder
Dessert: Vanilla Pudding with Brandied Cherries

Breakfast: Sunrise Bowl
Lunch: Orange Spiced Hummus, crackers, carrot sticks
Dinner: at home

Online Sources

Emergency Essentials
http://beprepared.com/

Harmony House Foods
http://www.harmonyhousefoods.com/

Just Tomatoes Etc.
http://www.justtomatoes.com/

King Arthur Flour
http://kingarthurflour.com/

Minimus
http://www.minimus.biz/

REI
http://www.rei.com/

True Lemon
http://www.truelemon.com/

Walton Feed
http://waltonfeed.com/

Index

About the Author

Teresa Black has been hiking and camping all over Washington since she was a child. She discovered backpacking in college, where she acquired the name "Dicentra". She is also the co-founder of a regional hiking group; the Pacific Northwest Hikers.

She attended the College of Forestry at the University of Washington and spent several summers working for Olympic National Park, which remains her favorite wilderness area to explore.

Teresa is a Washington native and lives in the Seattle area with her husband and daughter. In addition to cooking, both at home and on the trail, she enjoys botany, reading and photography.

More recipes, photos and information can be found at the One Pan Wonders website, http://www.onepanwonders.com

Teresa "Dicentra" Black can be contacted at dicentra@onepanwonders.com